A REVISED AND EXPANDED EDITION OF
Spiritual Quests: The Art and Craft of Religious Writing

Going on Faith

WRITING AS A SPIRITUAL QUEST

Edited and with an introduction by
William Zinsser

DIANE ACKERMAN
DAVID BRADLEY
FREDERICK BUECHNER
ALLEN GINSBERG
MARY GORDON
PATRICIA HAMPL
HILLEL LEVINE
HUGH NISSENSON
JAROSLAV PELIKAN

MARLOWE & COMPANY
NEW YORK

Published by
Marlowe & Company
841 Broadway, 4th Floor
New York, NY 10003

An earlier edition of this book was originally published in hardcover in 1988 by Houghton Mifflin Company under the title *Spiritual Quests: The Art and Craft of Religious Writing.*

Library of Congress Cataloging-in-Publication Data

Spiritual quests.
    Going on faith : writing as a spiritual quest / edited by William Zinsser.
        p. cm.
    Originally published: Spiritual quests. Boston : Houghton Mifflin, c1988.
    Includes bibliographical references.
    ISBN 1-56924-686-6
    1. Religious literature—Authorship. I. Zinsser, William Knowlton. II. Title.
    BR44.S62   1999
    808'.0662—dc21   98-52198
                                                        CIP

First Marlowe & Company printing, June 1999
Manufactured in the United States of America
Distributed by Publishers Group West

CONTENTS

WILLIAM ZINSSER

Introduction

One day in 1992 I got a call from the dean of the Earlham School of Religion, a division of Earlham College, a Quaker college in Indiana. He told me that his school was establishing a program called "The Ministry of Writing," and he asked if I would give the keynote talk. I said I would like nothing better. Then I asked: "How did you know?" How did he know that I've always regarded my writing as a form of ministry? I had never told anyone; I thought that would be presumptuous. He said: "It's all through your work."

That puzzled me, because it's not all through my work—not, at least, overtly. God turns up occasionally as a governing presence, and my sentences take some of their cadences and allusions from the King James Bible. But there's no mention of religious worship or religious belief—the residue of all those Sunday mornings spent in Protestant churches singing the hymns, reciting the Psalms and listening to the Word.

Yet on second thought I saw that the dean had me pegged. As a writer I try to operate within a framework of Christian principles, and the words that are important to me are religious words: witness, pilgrimage, intention. I think of intention as the writer's soul. Writers can write to affirm and to celebrate, or they can write to debunk and to destroy; the choice is ours. Editors may ask us to do destructive work for some purpose of their own, but nobody can make us write what we don't want to write. We get to keep intention.

I always write to affirm—or, if I start negatively, complaining about some situation or trend that strikes me as injurious, my goal is to arrive at a constructive point. I choose to write about people whose values I respect and who do life-affirming work; my pleasure is to bear witness to their lives. Much of my writing has taken the form of a pilgrimage: to sacred places that represent the best of America, to musicians and other artists who represent the best of their art.

My mother came from a long line of devout Maine and Connecticut Yankees, and she thought it was a Christian obligation to be cheerful. It is because of her that I am cursed with optimism. The belief that I can somehow will things to go right more often than they go wrong—or to be an agent of God's intention for them to go right—has brought many adjectives down on my head, none of them flattering: naive, credulous, simple-minded. All true. I plead guilty to positive thinking.

Whether this is a religious position I'll leave to some theologian. In any case, it's an act of faith—a challenge hurled in the face of the cynics. I like St. Paul's admonition: "Be not forgetful to entertain strangers: for thereby some have entertained angels unawares." I'm far more often surprised by grace than disappointed. I see too much goodness in everyday life, too many men and women and children going about God's work, not to want to hitch myself to that enterprise.

My penchant for subjects that involve a pilgrimage has often put me in the presence of a sacramental moment. Angels have caught me unawares in many parts of the world. I think of a Bedouin in the Sahara desert near Timbuktu who made me a gift of hospitality that I've never forgotten. I think of a Vietnamese poet in Hanoi who made me a gift of reconciliation that as an American I had never expected to deserve. I think of an ex-G.I. visiting the American cemetery at Omaha Beach who found absolution from memories he had kept repressed since June 6, 1944. I had gone there just before the 50th anniversary of D-Day to see if my generation of men had finally made peace with the war we fought when we were young.

I think of a Balinese drummer who came into my life without warning one night in 1952. Journalistic duty then required me to attend every Broadway opening, and I was sitting in the Fulton Theater waiting for a show called *Dancers of Bali* to begin. I had no idea what to expect; nowhere had my life or my education been touched by the cultures of Southeast Asia. The curtain went up and I heard a CLANG! that almost knocked me out of my seat. Twenty-five Balinese men were sitting cross-legged on the stage, striking an assortment of cymbals and gongs and xylophones with an intricacy of rhythm unlike anything I had ever heard. It was my first gamelan orchestra. Where had this wonderful sound been all my life? Although the scale had only five tones, the notes rose and fell in cascades of melody and counterpoint, sometimes reaching high intensity, sometimes turning slow and delicate. Yet no sign ever seemed to pass between the musicians and the dignified older man playing a drum who was obviously their leader.

I was further electrified when the dancers began to appear, costumed as princes and demons and dragons, presenting a succession of temple dances. They had an elegance of body movement and hand gesture that was new to me, and the program concluded with a classical *legong*, performed by three lithe little girls who were tightly wrapped in sarongs and seemed to have no bones. I learned from the *Playbill* that the troupe was from one village, called Peliatan, but that what I had seen was not unlike what I might see in any Balinese village. Art in Bali was an assumed possession; the language didn't even have a word for "art."

That was something I had to see, and the next summer I flew to Bali and went up into the hills to Peliatan and looked up the old drummer, whose name was Anak Agung Gde Madera. (Anak Agung is a princely title.) He told me that the troupe was not long back from its successful tour of America; they had played 14 cities. I asked him where the musicians and dancers were now. He said they were all back at their jobs, mostly in the rice fields. Would they be performing anywhere? Not this week; no temple dances were scheduled on Peliatan's religious calendar. I should try some other village.

That's when I learned the first rule of traveling in Bali: ask and you will hear about a temple ceremony somewhere. Village X is doing a *barong* this evening; village Y is doing a *baris* and a *kebyar* tomorrow. Night after night I sat in the courtyard of some Balinese village and watched the same dances I had seen on Broadway, exquisitely performed and accompanied on a full gamelan by men and women who during the day had been laborers. Children and chickens were everywhere. Mothers stood in a circle, holding their babies. The tales from the *Ramayana* and the movements of the dancers and the tinkling of the gamelan got absorbed almost from birth.

Another CLANG! went off in my head. I saw that religion and art were intertwined with life, not taught in separate buildings and special classrooms on designated days of the week, as they were in my culture. I envied that sacred unity, and after that I began to look for it in all my travels. I've felt the spirit at work in villages in Africa and Asia and Brazil where nothing in my genes or my upbringing had prepared me to feel the spirit at work.

In 1972 I went back to Bali and headed up to Peliatan. I wanted to find out whether the Anak Agung drummer was still alive. I asked some village boys, and they led me to a pavilion, and there he was, teaching the *legong* to a class of little girls. Twenty years had turned him gray, and he moved with the stiffness of old age. But he greeted me warmly, and we talked about the long-ago night on Broadway that had brought me to his village once before. Then he went back to work.

He lifted one of the girls and put her down so that her feet were on his feet, facing forward. Then he held her by her skinny wrists and began to perform the *legong*, humming the gamelan melody for that portion of the dance. Back and forth and sideways they moved in stylized steps, bending and leaning, starting and stopping, the girl's tiny feet riding wherever the big feet took her.

I could almost feel the rhythms being passed from one body to the other; the old man's face was so serious and tender. Then he gave the same lesson to the other little girls. They were all as serious as he was; there was no sense that this was a chore, or extra homework, or anything but life itself.

But it's not necessary to go to Bali and Timbuktu. Here in America I've found just as many manifestations of grace. In 1990 I went to Montgomery, Alabama, to see the newly dedicated memorial by Maya Lin to the men and women and children who were killed during the struggle for civil rights. Lin's earlier Vietnam Memorial, in Washington, was, to me, one of America's religious places. With that wall of incised names she enabled the American people to heal through their fingertips the wounds of a war that had torn the nation apart. Now she had turned her mind and her heart to the dead of the civil rights era, one of America's great religious movements, its roots going back to the early-nineteenth-century abolitionists, its prophet the great religious writer Abraham Lincoln. To this day Lincoln's Second Inaugural Address, echoing with wrathful Old and New Testament phrases, serving notice that the Civil War would end only when God wanted it to end ("the Almighty has His own purposes"), speaks to the sin of slavery in language more powerful than that of any American writer.

In Montgomery I was glad to find Maya Lin's memorial only a few blocks from the Dexter Avenue Baptist Church, where a twenty-five-year-old preacher, Martin Luther King, Jr., started it all. The memorial has two components. One is a wall of water falling over the words that King paraphrased from the Book of Amos in two historic speeches—his "I have a dream" speech in Washington and his speech at the start of the Montgomery bus boycott: "We will not be satisfied until justice rolls down like waters and righteousness like a mighty stream."

The other component is a large circular table of black granite. Carved into its top, around the perimeter, are fifty-three chronological entries naming and identifying people who were murdered in the South in the 1950s and '60s—typically, the four young girls who were bombed in a Birmingham church and the fourteen-year-old Emmett Till, who was killed for speaking to a white woman in Mississippi. A thin film of water flows over the tabletop. Most visitors walk slowly around the table, pausing to read and touch the names of the dead just beneath the water.

Afterward I asked Maya Lin how the idea for the memorial occurred to her. For several months, she told me, no ideas came at all. "The discipline is not to jump too fast," she said. "If you jump to a form too quickly it won't have the understood meaning you want for it." Finally the day arrived for her to fly to Montgomery to inspect the site, and it was on the plane, reading a book called *Eyes on the Prize*, that she came upon King's phrase about justice rolling down.

"The minute I hit that quote," she said, "I knew that the whole piece had to be about water." What she didn't anticipate was the power that words would generate when they were combined with water. "At the dedication ceremony," she told me, "I was surprised and moved when people started to cry. Emmett Till's mother was touching his name beneath the water and crying, and I realized that her tears were becoming part of the memorial."

Did Maya Lin describe that moment to any other writer? Did any other writer see the old Balinese drummer giving a *legong* lesson? Probably not. Why was I the chosen witness? Mathematically, the odds favored my being there; writers who go on spiritual quests put themselves in a position to observe spiritual transactions. But I could also argue that I was put there by God—a God who wants to make sure that His best stories get told.

It was my interest in the spiritual quests of writers that led to the birth of this book in its first incarnation. In 1985 the Book-of-the-Month Club, where I was an editor, launched an annual series of lectures, held at the New York Public Library, in which six writers talked about a particular area of the writer's craft. Biography was the subject of the first series, and I subsequently edited those six talks into a book called *Extraordinary Lives*. The next series was on memoir, which resulted in the book *Inventing the Truth*, which has since been expanded twice. Our speakers were asked to be specific and anecdotal—to explain how they went about their work—and they generously obliged. Biographers and memoirists as varied as David McCullough and Jean Strouse, Annie Dillard and Alfred Kazin, Russell Baker and Toni Morrison took us on deeply personal journeys, describing mountains laboriously scaled and trails mistakenly pursued.

By 1987 the series had developed a trusting audience, and I thought the moment was right to try a subject that was almost too private to discuss: religious writing. Writers who are nourished by spiritual concerns, it seemed to me, are on a different kind of pilgrimage from other writers: a lifelong search for the source of their faith as individuals and of their strength as artists. I wanted to hear about that search, and I invited six men and women from various points of God's compass.

Four of them were novelists: David Bradley (Methodist), Frederick Buechner (Presbyterian), Mary Gordon (Roman Catholic) and Hugh Nissenson (Jewish). One was the Jewish Buddhist poet Allen Ginsberg, and the sixth was the religious historian Jaroslav Pelikan, a scholar of the Middle Ages and the Reformation. The pilgrimages they told us about on those six winter evenings had nothing in common—the black Methodist preachers of David Bradley's Pennsylvania boyhood are more than a continent away from the Tibetan lamas who touched Allen Ginsberg with the notion of "spontaneous awareness." But when the talks were gathered under one roof, in the book *Spiritual Quests*, the same spirit ran through them all: a sense of the holy.

"I lean over backwards not to preach in my novels, because that would make for neither good novels nor good preaching," said Frederick Buechner, rejecting the label of "religious novelist" that has often been pinned on him in his long double career. A Presbyterian minister, he is the author of thirty books, one of which, *Godric*, a novel about a twelfth-century English saint, was nominated for the Pulitzer Prize.

"I'm a Christian writer in the sense that somebody from this country is an American writer; it's no more complicated or sinister than that," Buechner said. "Doubt and darkness have their say along with faith and hope in the books I write, because to do it any other way would diminish the richness of the experience I'm trying to be true to." His account of his creative process was full of uninvited visitors from a realm that may or may not have been coincidence, bearing gifts he wouldn't have found on his own. "Something outside ourselves is breathed into us," he said.

Mary Gordon's readers also tend to think of her as a religious novelist, or, rather, a Catholic novelist: her penalty for writing the hugely popular and hugely Catholic *Final Payments*. But like her literary forebears—Evelyn Waugh, for instance, and Graham Greene—she considers

11

herself a writer, not a Catholic writer. "Obviously the metaphors and concerns of my fiction have been shaped by the perspectives of Catholicism," she said, "but what interests me is how Catholicism provides both high esthetic standards and a closed (and enclosed) social system that are invaluable tools for a novelist."

Holiness first presented itself to Gordon in the form of symbols she repeatedly saw and heard as a child attending Mass ("the cruet's tinkle, the vestments' rustle"). All writers are voyeurs, she reminded us, and "to spend an hour a day in a confined space, where one has the leisure or the boredom to observe others of one's kind when they imagine themselves to be in private communion with their deepest thoughts, is as useful for a prospective novelist as a wiretap." The Mass was also a lesson in structure—a narrative drama building to a central event—and in the grandeur and variety of the spoken word. "There is," she said, "a regular alternation of levels of language and types of literature," ranging from scriptural invocation and reflective prayer to Old Testament narratives and the poetry of the Psalms.

In the case of David Bradley, whose novel *The Chaneysville Incident* established him as a major black American writer, religion came with the family; he was born plugged into one of the most lively currents of American Protestantism. "Much of what I do, and the way in which I try to do it," he said, "is influenced by the fact that I come from a long line of preachers. My father, my grandfather and my great-grandfather, a freedman, were all ministers in the African Methodist Episcopal Zion Church, and as a boy I led many services myself. I think of the act of writing as a worship service—not only for the reader, but for the writer."

Hugh Nissenson, author of four books of Jewish experience, caught his followers off balance in the mid-1980s with *The Tree of Life*, a novel about Protestants on the Ohio frontier. He insisted, however, that the book wasn't a freakish detour, but part of a longer journey. "Together," he said, "my books form a spiritual autobiography reflecting my obsession with religious experience. All my life I've been on a quest for the source of the mysteries that inspire me. It's interesting that the Jews gave Christianity the idea that the word becomes God: that the word itself is God, that it's inextricably intertwined with the Creator."

Allen Ginsberg had long been on a similar pilgrimage. One of the most influential literary voices of his generation, Ginsberg, who died in 1997, sought out the religions of the East as an artistic and a spiritual source in the 1960s and not long afterward took up the study and practice of Buddhist meditation. He considered his poetry and his religion inseparable, he said, referring to "the surprise glimpse of sudden insight" that can come from an unexpected source "when an intervening veil of preconceived ideas" is removed. His talk was a litany of metaphysical poets whispering, if not shouting, in his ear.

Jaroslav Pelikan's quest had been the longest of all, both in historical time and in writer's time: his five-volume *The Christian Tradition*, a study of the development of Christian doctrine, occupied him for more than forty years. "That task," he said, "has forced me to acquire an antenna for a great variety of religious signals sent out by gnostics and scholastics, mystics and reformers." Now, asked to give a talk on religious writing, he spoke about the three men he regards as the fathers of the form: Augustine, whose *Confessions*, "one of the few books from antiquity that have never gone out of style," is "one single uninterrupted sentence, addressed to

God"; John Henry Newman, whose *Apologia Pro Vita Sua* was "a quest to understand the mystery of his conversion and to communicate it in a way that others will, if not understand, at least respect and forgive"; and Boethius, the sixth-century Roman author of *The Consolation of Philosophy*, who used the experience of his imprisonment "to explore within himself the resources of insight, faith and hope." All three writers, Pelikan noted, "made themselves the object of their own study and thereby made their writing a means of grace for themselves and for others."

So *Spiritual Quests* went forth with these six voyagers in 1988. It found a devoted audience of writers, teachers and assorted seekers and finally went out of print. In 1998 I was approached by another publisher, who wanted to reissue the book, adding new writers to the original mix.

His idea appealed to me. The winds of a religious revival were blowing through bookstores across America at the end of the century: a new interest in matters of the spirit. I also welcomed the opportunity to make the book broader—to include quests that weren't represented in the first edition—and I enlisted Diane Ackerman, Patricia Hampl and Hillel Levine. To preserve the oral integrity of the book as a collection of talks I went to those three writers with my tape recorder, eliciting their story and then editing the transcript into a narrative. The book also got a new title: *Going on Faith*.

What I had most missed in the first edition was a Jewish writer talking out of a lifelong spiritual search. Surveying the work of modern Jewish authors, I found almost no candidates—writers who actually discussed religious belief. They tended to honor secular gods—gods of the mind—and I couldn't argue with that; the intellectual and artistic attainments of the Jews have enriched America beyond measure. Only when they wrote about the Holocaust, I felt, did most modern Jewish writers seem to tackle a subject that might partake of the spiritual. Was the Holocaust, perhaps, a modern surrogate for religion?

I wanted a writer who could address the enigma of the Holocaust out of the wellsprings of Judaic faith. My thoughts turned to Hillel Levine, whose book, *In Search of Sugihara*, is a pilgrimage to the story of the Japanese diplomat in Lithuania who, for no apparent reason, saved as many as ten thousand Jews on the eve of World War II by giving them exit visas. I first knew Hillel Levine when we were both teaching at Yale many years ago. A rabbi by training and a sociologist by vocation, a man of deep faith, he taught a popular course called "the sociology of evil," in which he searched for the mystery of the evil that almost exterminated his people in Europe. That search took a 180-degree turn one day in the early 1990s, when he remembered the story of Sugihara and felt a prophetic call to go in search of the mystery of goodness.

How he heard that call as he stood outside the former Japanese consulate in Kovno, frozen by a vision of the hand of Sugihara signing visas, is part of the spiritual journey that Levine retraces here, starting when he became a teenage wanderer, traveling "to places where people in their junior year abroad don't go, visiting the graveyards of Jewish life, looking for what I knew no longer existed." The journey reaches a climax thirty years later when he tracks down Sugihara's 93-year-old first wife in a nursing home in Australia. Three days after telling him what he needed to know about Sugihara—that he was a man of essential goodness—she died. "It was as if she had been waiting for me all those years."

Diane Ackerman was my choice for a writer who finds religion everywhere except in churches; she doesn't believe in organized worship or a ruling God. Her beat is the universe, and her wonder is at the sanctity of all life; she thinks of herself as an "earth ecstatic." Her pursuit of that creed has taken her to many remote parts of the world to write about creatures living on the edge of extinction. One expedition, described here, brought her to a tiny volcanic island off Japan to observe the last of the short-tailed albatrosses, their nesting place reachable only after a 400-foot rope descent that left her with three broken ribs. At the bottom of the cliff she sat for two days, unable to move but grateful for the view. "There is a form of beholding that is a kind of prayer," she says. "I wanted to celebrate the birds. I didn't want them to die without someone bearing witness to how extraordinary they are."

Today it is the fragility of the human animal that Ackerman witnesses in her writing, she says, recalling how her book *A Slender Thread* grew out of a five-year stint on a suicide-prevention hotline. That work disclosed a number of affinities between man and the natural species she had previously studied. "I may seem to have written many books, but it's always the same book, the same puzzle."

The third new writer I recruited was Patricia Hampl, author of a memoir that I admired as still another kind of religious quest: *Virgin Time: In Search of the Contemplative Life.* Hampl describes her constricted Roman Catholic girlhood in Minnesota and the seeds of faith that it planted, which would push her, half a lifetime later, to explore the life of religious contemplation, first in a Franciscan monastery in Assisi and then at a silent cloistered retreat in northern California. It was language, she recalls here, that first drew her into "the inevitable human drama that people call spirituality." Specifically, it was the Psalms, speaking to her across the ages about all the "love, betrayal, rancor, joy, radiance, misery, fury and pettiness" of human experience.

In the end Hampl found that monastic life was like stepping through a mirror, altering her assumptions. "Going on retreat," she says, "is the inverse of going on pilgrimage. On a pilgrimage you're going forward, you're seeking. On retreat you're backing off and letting something come at you. I now feel that everything eventually returns to silence. There's an instinct towards the kind of silence that's in the middle of prayer. The whole point of contemplative life is the reaching out that goes just beyond articulation."

So my expanded lineup fell into place. The result is a book of stories, told with joy and gratitude. Listen and you will hear nine writers going on faith. Faith is the adrenaline of every spiritually inclined writer, and none of us, I suspect, would trade it for any steroid claiming to be stronger.

MARY GORDON

*Getting Here from There:
A Writer's Reflections on a
Religious Past*

To begin speaking about the words "spiritual quests" in relation to myself fills me simultaneously with amusement and alarm. Amusement because the words "spiritual" and "quest" conjure up the imagery of the knight consecrate, Galahad after the Holy Grail, dying picturesquely at the very moment he fulfills his goal. I can't see myself in the part. And alarm because the very word "spiritual" suggests to me the twin dangers of the religious life: dualism and abstraction.

Abstractionism I define as the error that results from refusing to admit that one has a body and is an inhabitant of the physical world. Dualism, its first cousin, admits that there is a physical world but calls it evil and commands that it be shunned. I'd venture to say that these two what I call "sins"—dualism and abstraction—are the cause of at least as much human misery as pride, covetousness, lust, envy, hatred, gluttony and sloth. Those names come very easily to my mind—names learned in childhood, memorized in childhood. They're one of those lists, those catalogues, that made the blood race with the buildup. So many catalogues there were in the church I grew up in, so many lists: seven capital sins, three theological virtues and four moral ones, seven sacraments, seven gifts of the Holy Ghost. A kind of poetry of accumulation, gaining power like an avalanche from its own momentum—perhaps a small influence, but in my prose an important one that I grew up hearing every day of my life, for my childhood days were shaped and marked by the religious devotions of my parents, by the rhythmic, repetitive cadences of formal prayer. It bred in me a love for strongly rhythmic prose.

I can never talk about the spiritual or the religious life without talking about early memory, which is anything but disembodied. Whatever religious instincts I have bring their messages to me through the senses—the images of my religious life, its sounds, its odors, the kind of kinesthetic sense I have of prayerfulness. These are much more real to me than anything that takes place in the life of the mind. I want to say that I've never been drawn to any kind of systematic theology except as a kind of curiosity, though as soon as I say this I want to qualify it, because what makes me even more nervous than the word "spiritual" are the words "evangelical," or "charismatic." The religious impulse unmediated by reason terrifies me, and it seems to me that we are always having to mediate between the emotions, the body, the reason. So even though I can't be moved forward in any way by systematic theology, I like it to be there, in the same way that I like modern architecture to be there, even though I don't want to live in it.

And the body must be not be left out. I was born into

a church shaped and ruled by celibate males who had a history of hatred and fear of the body, which they lived out in their lives and in the rituals they invented. They excluded women from the center of their official and their personal lives. When I tried to think of any rituals that acknowledged the body, except for rituals involving death and in a very oblique way birth, the only one I could think of was what used to be called "the churching of women," which is a blessing for the mother, a kind of purification after the mess of birth. It's a remembrance of the purification of the Virgin Mary; she would have been actually submerged in water, not merely symbolically cleansed, for the reentry into the legitimate world where body life could once again be hidden.

I keep having to backtrack; every time I say something I instantly think that I haven't quite told the truth, because I have to confess and acknowledge my own dualism. Much of what is beautiful to me in my religious experience is its bodylessness. I remember the early morning Masses of my childhood. In my memory the atmosphere is always gray, a kind of false dawn, air without heat or light. I'm walking with one of my parents, never both, because these memories are the *tête à têtes* of the anointed "only child," the child of parents who preferred her to each other. The women in my memories are wearing coats of muted colors, kerchiefs, round-toed nun-like shoes. The nuns themselves are disappearing in their habits, faceless. They are only forms. The church is coldish. It is silent. In the sacristy you can hear the mysterious, inexplicable, untraceable noises of the priest and the altar boy—the cruet's tinkle, the vestments' rustle. There are whispered words.

And then there is the Mass. In preparing this talk, it occurred to me for the first time what an excellent training ground the regular attendance at Mass was for an aspiring novelist. First, there's the form of the Mass itself, which popularly has been compared to drama, but the likenesses with the novel are also not at all unapt. The central event of the Mass occurs—interestingly for the novelist, I think—way past its middle. It's the consecration, the turning of bread and wine into the body and blood of Christ. I have to say a word about this, because for orthodox Catholics this is an actual transformation of substance. (The doctrine is called transubstantiation.) That is to say, for an orthodox Catholic the bread and wine is no longer believed to be bread and wine; it has changed in its essence, in what the scholastic philosophers called its substance, so that it is no longer bread and wine but has been actually transformed into the body and blood of Christ. Somewhere there's a conversation I like between Mary McCarthy and Flannery O'Connor in which Mary McCarthy tries to get Flannery O'Connor to admit that she really believes that transubstantiation is only a symbolic act. And Flannery O'Connor is reported to have said, "If I thought it were just a symbol I'd say the hell with it."

For the novelist, then, there is a central dramatic event. But, interestingly, there is also a regular alternation of levels of language and types of literature within the Mass itself. There's scriptural invocation, reflective prayer, the poetry of the Psalms, the Old Testament and Gospel narratives and the repetitions: the Sanctus, the Agnus Dei, the *Domini non sum dignus*, repeated three times, the first and last time to the accompaniment of bells. Different types of Masses offer to the sensitive ear examples of different kinds of formality and embellishment, from the simple daily Low Mass to the more formal Sunday Low Mass to the High Mass, complete with choirs, chants and all the liturgical stops pulled out.

I'm not saying that as a child I consciously understood this. Obviously I didn't. As a matter of fact, I don't think I thought of it at all until I was preparing this talk. But I absorbed it unconsciously, this elaborate and varied and supple use of language. From a very early age it wove itself into my bones. Once again, Flannery O'Connor says that the writer learns everything important to him or her before the age of six. So every day, for however often I was taken to daily Mass, I was learning lessons in rhetoric.

And I was also learning a lot of other things. If we accept the truism that all writers are voyeurs, then we can say that an hour a day in a confined space like a church, where one has the leisure or the boredom to observe others of one's kind when they imagine themselves to be in private communion with their deepest souls, is as useful for a prospective novelist as a wiretap. Daily Mass was the home ground of the marginal, the underemployed; you always wondered why they weren't at work or getting ready for work. A child at daily Mass got to observe at close range the habits of old women, of housewives at eight-thirty already tired out for the day, men down on their luck praying for a reversal of their bad fortunes.

You also got wonderful lessons in structure. The structure of the Mass, like that of the parish, composed itself around the figure of the priest, the center of all our earthly attentions, the center of parish life, at an observable distance on the altar for an hour of our time. The erotically charged yet unreachable figure of the priest! And around him, theoretically invisible, and yet of course the pulse of parish life, the women: jockeying, serving (except on the altar, where they were forbidden to be), dreaming, losing and gaining lives against the backdrop of history. And the single figure of the priest, who could contain in himself the whole world. The priest was theoretically available to all, and yet available to no one, just as the Church was in theory open to all and in theory welcoming of all, but in fact operated on principles of initiation and exclusion. For all that, it has always contained a membership that includes representatives from all of Europe and all the places where the Europeans set down their iron-shod feet.

So to be a Catholic, or even to have been one, is to feel a certain access to a world wider than the vision allowed by the lens of one's own birth. You grew up believing that the parish is the world, and that anyone in the world could be a member of the parish. But of course the parish was a fiercely limited terrain: the perfect size and conformation for the study of the future novelist. Anachronistically limited, its hierarchies clear, its loyalties assumed and stated and then in practice always undermined, it has at its center issues of money. You learned from the parish how the watermarks of class and privilege work. You could see how the impressive personality, the personality of the clergy, can change life.

A novelist builds a fence enclosing a certain area of the world and then calls it his or her subject. To be a Catholic, particularly in Protestant America, made one an expert at building the limiting, excluding fence. Inside the paddock there were shared assumptions about everything from the appropriate postures for kneeling to the nature of human consciousness. But there was always a right way and a wrong way, and you always knew which was which.

One could be, at least in the time when I was growing up, a Catholic in New York and deal only in the most superficial of ways with anyone non-Catholic. Until I went to college I had no genuine contact with anyone who wasn't Catholic. The tailor and the man who ran the candy store were Jews, and the women who worked in the public library were Protestants, but you only allowed them the pleasantries. Real life, the friendships, the feuds, the passions of proximate existence, took place in the sectarian compound, a compound, like any other, with its secrets—a secret language, secret customs, rites, which I now understand must have been very menacing at worst or at the best puzzling to the outside world.

But we never knew that, because we never understood that the rest of the world was looking. We weren't interested in the rest of the world. If some of us did assume that the rest of the world was looking, our response was to be all the more zealous in keeping the secrets secret. One of the greatest treasures a novelist can have is a secret world which he or she can open up to his or her reader. When I turned from poetry to fiction in my mid-twenties, I had a natural subject—the secrets of the Catholic world. And since the door had not been very widely opened before I got there, I was a natural. I think that accounts to a great extent for the popularity of *Final Payments*.

Now we're going to descend into autobiography. I don't know how successful I can be in conveying the extent to which my family life was shaped by Catholicism. My parents' whole marriage was based on it; it was literally the only thing they had in common. My father was an intellectual Jew, who had had a very wild life. And simply to give you the outlines of it will give you a sense of its wildness. He was born in Lorain, Ohio. He also lied a lot, so it's extremely hard to trace what's the truth. I think this is the truth; at least I'm not consciously passing on lies. But it could *not* be the truth. So I possibly have a great-grandfather who was a rabbi, but my father also said that his mother was a concert pianist, and who knows? He told me, for example, that his father ran a saloon; in fact, he ran a dry goods store.

In any case, my father went to Harvard in 1917. At that time there was a rigid quota system for Jews, and I think it must have caused him tremendous pain. Because what I think is that at Harvard he determined to "pass" at any cost. And my father, who was endlessly inventive, figured out that the best way for a Jew to pass was to be right-wing. My father became righter-wing than anybody, with a couple of interesting pit stops. For example, he went to Paris and England for a while in the twenties. And one persona that he created for some reason was to pass himself off as a Middle West Presbyterian. He looked a lot like me—I don't know why anybody believed him. Maybe they thought all Americans look alike. He wrote a series of articles in English journals, passing himself off as a Midwest Protestant who understands that Europe is really a superior culture to his own. It's very strange.

His other pit stop was also in the late twenties. He published a girlie magazine called *Hot Dog*. I remember being twelve, and my father had died when I was seven, and I came upon this magazine while looking through his pictures. By today's standards it's exceedingly mild. But I was an exceedingly prudish twelve-year-old, and I took a look at this thing and I saw that my father had been the editor, and I was appalled and I ripped it to shreds and threw it away. So I have no record of it. But I'm pretty sure I didn't make it up.

In any case, my father became a Francoist in the thirties. You rarely meet somebody who can say that sentence—everybody else's father was in the Lincoln

Brigade. Not mine. And in the course of several later adventures he met my mother. They met through a priest. My mother is the daughter of very simple Irish and Italian Catholics. I think she embodied for my father a kind of peasant Catholicism that he romanticized. But both of them could say with truthfulness that their faith was the most important thing in the world to them.

From an early age I had to take the measure of myself against their devotedness, and I always found myself wanting. Throughout my childhood I prayed to be spared martyrdom. But then I always felt guilty for the prayer. I was no little Teresa of Ávila setting out in the desert hoping to convert the Moors; the priests in China having bamboo shoved under their fingernails and Cardinal Mindszenty imprisoned in his upper room terrified me. I didn't want that for my fate, but I was told that it was the highest fate. So as a child I had to always be consciously choosing an inferior fate. It was a real burden.

But I do remember that although I didn't want to be a martyr, I did want to be a nun. I remember being taken by my parents to the Convent of Mary Reperatrix on Twenty-ninth Street. It's a semi-cloistered convent—the nuns weren't allowed out, but people could talk to them. And I remember going into the chapel with my parents and a very old nun. I saw a young nun kneeling in a pool of light. I saw her from the back only. The habits of the Sisters of Mary Reperatrix were sky-blue. I've never seen a color like that in a nun's habit, and I'm quite sure I didn't invent it. But if I had wanted to invent it, it would have been perfect because it was a color dreamed up for movie stars. It was the color of Sleeping Beauty's ball gown, and that was what I wanted for myself. I wanted to be beautifully kneeling in light, my young, straight back clothed in the magic garment of the anointed. I knew that was what I wanted, but I knew I didn't want to drink filthy water or walk barefoot in the snow. But a few times I did try some local freelance missionary work.

Once, for instance, I had just finished reading the life of Saint Dominic Savio, who was a Neapolitan orphan. I was about six or seven. Saint Dominic walked into a playground and heard his rough playmates—isn't that wonderful; nobody uses the phrase "rough playmates" anymore—using blasphemous language. And he didn't skip a beat. He held up a crucifix and he said to those boys, "Say it in front of Him." And the boys fell silent. Inspired, I tried the same thing in my neighborhood. I walked into the crowd of boys with my crucifix aloft and I said, "Say it in front of Him." And they were glad to.

The comedy of Catholic life. It comes, of course, like all other comedy, from the gap between the ideal and the real. In my case the ideal was so high and the real was so real that the collision was bound to be risible. I tried walking with thorns in my shoes for penance, but then I found out that it hurt. So I walked around on the heels of my shoes and put the thorns in the toes, so I could have them in my shoes but not feel them. My heroisms were always compromised and always unsuccessful. I tried to talk the man in our gas station into taking the nude calendar off his wall. He told me never to come into the office again. I tried to make the candy store man, whom I genuinely liked, stop selling dirty magazines. He stopped giving me free egg creams, and our friendship ended. But he went right on selling dirty magazines.

I always tried. The serious part of the ideals that shaped my early life was that they did teach me that life was serious. I think all children believe that. I think parents cheat children by refusing to understand that everything is serious to them and that it is the modulations of the adult world that cause them such confused grief. At a very early age I was taught that happiness was not important; what was important was to save my soul. I was not supposed to be only a good girl or even a lady, although I was supposed to begin there. I was not supposed to even strive to be popular, successful, beloved, or valued by the world. I was supposed to be a saint. The cautionary and inspirational tales of my youth were the lives of the saints.

The lives of the saints. I recently took down a saints' lives book that was mine as a child. I sometimes read it to my children today. To my children these people—Saint Barnabus who juggled, Saint Nicholas who found children pickled in the basement of an inn and brought them back to life—are fairy-tale characters. They're characters like Ali Baba or Rapunzel. My daughter likes the picture of the boy child Saint Hugh kicking the devil downstairs. She asks me if the devil is real. And I tell her, "No, no, he's not real; he's like the banshee or the Loch Ness monster." And as I tell her that, I realize that for me the devil *was* real. And he was feared. My mother cured me of early narcissism by telling me that if I kept looking in the mirror the devil would pop out behind me, and that when I was looking at my face it would turn into the face of the devil. Well, I stopped immediately. I was talking about eternal life, and so was she, and we couldn't afford to take the risk.

There's a sentence in the incomparable story by Delmore Schwartz, "In Dreams Begin Responsibilities," in which the boy says, "Everything you do matters too much." Did everything matter too much for me? I'm not sure. But at least it mattered. What you learned with a background like mine was that everything mattered terribly and that you could never do enough.

I remember a friend of mine, a Jew, telling me he felt sorry for Christians because if you took seriously the words of Christ, "Greater love hath no man than this, that a man lay down his life for his friends," then as long as you were alive you hadn't done enough. But this is not such a bad thing for an artist. For the life of the working artist is a perpetual reminder that everything you do matters. Nothing is enough.

Speaking of the lives of the saints makes me try to differentiate among the kinds of narratives that a pious Catholic child encountered. There were the Old Testament narratives, which always seemed to me forbidding and harsh and frightening—exciting as war movies were exciting and dangerous, but of no comfort. Abraham and Isaac, Moses left in the bulrushes, Joseph thrown down the well by his brothers, the boy David all alone with a slingshot—you had the vision of children for whom the adult world offered no protection. There were the failing parents and the implacable voice of God. I always felt as if the narratives of the Old Testament were accompanied by a kind of rumble. The colors were dark and vibrant. I was drawn to them, but I wanted to get away. To Jesus and the children.

I remember a jigsaw puzzle I had of Jesus and the children: the warm, inviting lap, the face of infinite acceptance. And there were the other images—the prodigal son forgiven, the daughter of Gyrus raised, the blind given his sight, the lame his nimbleness, the good thief ushered into paradise. But there was also a disturbing underside of New Testament violence. It was disturbing in a way that Old Testament violence was not, because in the old narratives the violence all seemed of a piece with the rest of the vision of the world, whereas in the Gospels it was always a surprise and something of a cheat. It was the terrible massacre of the innocents, the beheading of John the Baptist, the sufferings and death of Christ himself—somehow the triumph always paid for by some ancillary, unwilled or only partially willed carnage. Easter paid for by Lent. How fully I lived my childhood Holy Weeks, the most solemn time of the year, religiously then as now my favorite! The black vestments, the stripped altar, the shocked silence of the congregation and then the midnight fire and the morning promise of Easter. In my memory Easter was always warm; you could always wear your spring coat and your straw hat, although in my adulthood more than half the Easters have been covered in snow.

The third kind of narrative, the lives of the saints, were magical in ways that the Bible of both Testaments was too austere to permit. Saint Francis talked to birds and wolves. Saint Elizabeth of Hungary, a queen, carried bread to the poor and the plague-ridden, although her husband the king had forbidden it. She hid the bread in her apron to keep it from the eyes of her husband and the palace guards. Her husband the king found out; he confronted her with his soldiers at the castle gate, demanding that she show him what was inside her apron. She opened her apron, and where there had been bread there were roses. He fell on his knees before his wife.

It occurs to me that one good fortune in being brought up a Catholic and a woman was that you did have images of heroic women. And that's not so frequently the case in other religious traditions. In the tradition of Catholicism you have a poem spoken by the Virgin Mary which points out her place in the divine order. And she speaks with pride. She says, "My soul doth magnify the Lord and my spirit hath rejoiced in God, my saviour. Because He has regarded the loneliness of His handmaid, and behold from henceforth all generations shall call me blessed, for He that is mighty hath done great things to me and holy is His name." That's an example of a woman's speech and a woman acknowledging her importance in the hierarchy, which at least in some subliminal way a girl got to hold onto.

In the lives of the saints you had a lot of examples of women who defined themselves not in terms of men but in terms of each other. You had the founders of orders. You had women who defied the Pope, defied the bishops, to go off and do things that women were not supposed to do. You had "doctors of the church"—women saints who were given that title. Did I know at age five what that meant—"doctor of the church"? Not exactly. But there was something there. You had an image of an alternate female world that often had to trick the male world in the same way that Saint Elizabeth had to trick her husband the king. A lot of women have survived through trickery. It was not entirely a bad life, but I hope it's one we can soon forget. Still, it wasn't a bad arrow to have in your quiver.

The saints came in various personality types. There was the meek Little Flower and the fierce Spanish Teresa. There was Saint Jerome in the desert with his blood-red eyes and the Curé of Ars, the friend of everybody in his little village. There were monks and scholars, widows and virgins, popes and ferrymen. I've stopped doing missionary work among the candy store owners of the world, but one of my missionary works is to try to remind people of wonderful woman writers who are undernoticed and often out of print. Louise Bogan, I think, is an exquisite poet—as good as anybody who has written in this century. Except for one small collection, her work is out of print, so I'm taking this opportunity to get you to create a great stir to get Louise Bogan back. I'll read you a poem of hers called "Saint Christopher," since we're talking about saints' lives and I think it will give you something of the flavor of those lives, which were so wonderful for a child to hear and get from them a sense of narrative:

A raw-boned and an ignorant man
Keeps ferry, but a man of nerve,
His freight a Child and a Child's toy.
(Which is our globe, you will observe.)

But what a look of intent love!
This is the look we do not see
In manners or in mimicry.
Strength's a derivative thereof.

The middle class is what we are.
Poised as a brigand or a barber
The tough young saint, Saint Christopher,
Brings the Child into the safe harbor.

Among all these saints, among all the types that were represented and honored, there are no artists, unless you count Saint Francis de Sales, who is the patron saint of writers, and he was hardly what we would call a creative writer; he was a composer of meditations. From the way I've described the riches of the Catholic background you may think it would be almost inevitable that any pious child would grow up to be an artist. But as a group, Catholics—particularly Catholics in America and even ex-Catholics—are scandalously underrepresented in the arts. I'm always surprised by this, but I shouldn't be. The orthodox have no need of consolation, and a closed world has no need of descriptions of itself. For a Catholic who took the teachings of the Church seriously, art for art's sake is as foreign as the idea of a Moslem heaven. Even knowledge was not encouraged for its own sake, but in the service of God. I've just gone through an old prayer book of my mother's, which I used to read a lot as a child. And I came across these prayers which I thought would illustrate for you what I'm trying to say about the notion that the life of the mind was never for itself but always in the service of God.

This first prayer is a prayer to Saint Catherine of Siena, who was a doctor of the church. It goes:

> Oh, glorious Saint Catherine, wise and prudent virgin, Thou who didst set the knowledge of Jesus Christ above all other knowledge. Obtain for us the grace to remain inviolably attached to the Catholic faith and to seek in our studies and in our teaching only the extension of the kingdom of Jesus Christ our Lord and of His holy church, both in our selves and in the souls of others. Amen.

The second prayer is a prayer to the Virgin Mary, which is supposed to be said by students:

> Under thy patronage, Dear Mother, and invoking the mystery of thine immaculate conception, I desire to pursue my studies and my literary labors. I hereby solemnly declare that I am devoting myself to these studies chiefly to the following end: That I may the better contribute to the glory of God and to the spread of thy veneration among men. I pray thee, therefore, most loving mother, who art the seat of

wisdom, to bless my labors in thy loving kindness. Moreover, I promise with true affection and a waking spirit, as it is right that I should do, to ascribe all the good that shall accrue to me therefrom wholly to thine intercession for me in God's holy presence. Amen.

Nobody walking fully under the banner represented by those prayers could create a modern work of art. The artistic ego, a product of the Renaissance, coincided with the loosening of the grip of the Church over the hearts and minds of women and men. The enclosed garden of my childhood was enclosed by a system that said all acts found their meaning in the reiteration of the Truth. Capital T. Whereas that might have been a vessel of inspiration for the author of *The Divine Comedy* or the *Pange Lingua,* it could be of no help to a modern artist, particularly a novelist whose origins are in the secular mind of the eighteenth century.

When you're talking about the Catholic Church you always have to go back and forth between the levels of the spiritual, the private, the ideal and the real. Because the Catholic Church, for better and for worse, is a worldwide church that encompasses races and classes of all sorts. And I think that the silence of American Catholics in relation to the arts is an accident of class, ethnicity and history as much as it is of spiritual over-idealism. I think we have to remember that the Catholic Church in America is the Irish Church. And the Irish Church is a church that is obsessed and committed to the idea of keeping silence. There's a famous Irish expression: "An Irish person will tell you something, and then they'll say, 'Mind you, I've said nothing.' "

The book I'm writing now is very much about Irish

immigration, so I'm reading a lot about the Irish, and I've had the funny experience of listening to researchers who have done oral histories of the Irish. And I can tell they're not Irish themselves. They go into nursing homes, where people have nothing to do—they're a captive audience—and the interviewers ask questions and ask questions and these old people answer with tremendous politeness and a great flurry of language and convey absolutely no information.

People always say, "Well, the Irish are so garrulous. They love to talk." They love to talk, but they don't like to tell you anything. So if you're happy to have a good time and listen to the shape of the language itself you'll have a wonderful time talking to an Irishman. If you want to know anything about his or her life, forget it. People say, "Well, he'll get drunk and . . ." Nothing. That has nothing to do with it. You will not get at the truth. The Irish are obsessed with concealing the inner life.

I think this is another reason why there has been such a silence, such an absence of the Catholic voice, in America. There's a lot of talk about the Irish Renaissance in Ireland. But those are not Catholic writers; you're talking about English Protestants who happened to set down roots and then get romantic about the auld sod. Nothing made Joyce more crazy than to hear Yeats carrying on about the Celtic twilight. And Yeats, of course, couldn't stand the Irish that he came in contact with. He wanted to fantasize about them heroically, but if he happened to meet one of his workmen in front of the tower he'd just as soon send him to jail as invite him in to dinner. So when you're talking about the Irish and about Catholicism in America and the presence of the arts, you have to talk about the presence of the Irish, which adds a lot of complications.

*   *   *

Well, how did I get from there to here? An easy answer would be that I substituted art for faith, so that I found my new priesthood. That would be an easy answer, but it's not true. I don't believe in the religion of art, although I do believe in the vocation of the artist—altogether a more slogging enterprise. I don't believe that the esthetic and the religious are one. To my mind, an experience to be properly religious must include three things: an ethical component, the possibility of full participation by the entire human community and acknowledgment of the existence of a life beyond the human. Art need do none of these things, although it may. Most art does not suggest a life beyond the human, unless you want to say that all inspiration is beyond the human and therefore it acknowledges it tacitly. I think that's fudging the question. There can be all sorts of sources of inspiration. They need not be personal; they need not be supra-human or extra-human.

And even the greatest art, even the greatest art when it is the simplest art, requires a certain prior cluing-in, a kind of training, however informal, in the rudiments of the art. Great art need have nothing in it of the ethical, although the greatness of some great literature is enhanced by ethical components. But some is not. And certainly it would be absurd to make those claims for painting or music. This is why I say that the esthetic and the religious are not necessarily one.

So how did I get there from here? How did I get here from there? You may notice that when I speak of religious influences I speak of the memories of childhood. When I was fourteen the Second Vatican Council began. Virginia Woolf tells us that on or about December, 1910, the world changed. Well, the great changes in the Church

39

coincided—unfortunately, perhaps—with the great changes in my body. I became at puberty properly irreligious, and I say "properly" with great advisement. I think one should beware of the religious adolescent; he may be planning your assassination in the night. I was fourteen when one of the greatest events in the Church's history took place. I'm reminded, again—a bit irrelevantly but not unpleasantly, I hope—of a poem, by Stevie Smith, called "The Conventionalist":

> *Fourteen-year-old, why must you giggle and dote?*
> *Fourteen-year-old, why are you such a goat?*
> *I'm fourteen years old, that is the reason.*
> *I giggle and dote in season.*

I'm afraid I was giggling and doting when Pope John was opening the windows of the Church. And the outside world beckoned me with much more force than the confused and angry Church of the early and mid-sixties. It's always amusing to me to talk to non-Catholics about their fantasy of what the Second Vatican Council did. They all imagine that we were clapping and singing and shouting "Hallelujah!" Most people were furious. Most people were confused and angry and outraged. They felt that the rug had been taken out from under them, particularly if they grew up as I did in a working-class neighborhood. There was no great sense of jubilation. It was a lucky thing for Pope John that he died; he got to look good, like John Kennedy.

It was at that point that I began to think of myself as a poet, as an artist. I had no more interest in being a saint. And a good thing, too—I stopped trying to get people to not sell magazines and I stopped putting thorns in my shoes. When I looked back over my shoulder to see what they were doing in the open-windowed Church, the part of me that was learning about great art could only run away. People were playing guitars at Mass now and re-writing Peter, Paul and Mary tunes to express Church dogma. If you'll forgive my bursting into song [sings]:

Take this bread
And take this wine
And take our hearts
And take our minds
At this Eucharistic feast
We are all priests.

I was fourteen. What could I do?

Well, it's fun to make fun of these excesses. I like doing it very much. But I don't think the answer is to turn the clock back. I don't want it turned back, because the people who are plumping for the reintroduction of Gregorian chant into the liturgy are also funding the Contras in Nicaragua, and they're doing it for the same reason. But I am grieved every time I enter a parish church and hear an unlovely liturgy, and I often have to leave for my own protection. I'm in a queer position: the Church of my childhood that was so important for my formation as an artist is now gone. As Gertrude Stein said of Oakland, "There is no there there."

But there *is* something there, something that formed me and that touches me still: the example of the nuns killed in El Salvador, of liberation theologians standing up to the Pope, of the nuns—the "Vatican 24"—who signed the statement asserting that it was possible for Catholics to have different positions on abortion and still be Catholics. These sisters, many of them in their sixties and seventies, faced the loss of everything—their sisterhood, their community, their lives, and things we wouldn't think of, like their medical insurance. They had no Social Security; they had no pension plans; they faced literally being thrown out on the street. They are extraordinary women.

These people whom I am moved by and whom I admire are nevertheless people who are very different from me. And what I admire in them is at a very great remove from the world of literature and art. Nevertheless I can't quite give up what they stand for. I don't want to give it up because I don't want to give it over to John Cardinal O'Connor and his kind.

So what do I do? I write my fictions. And my relation to the "there" that is not there I make up each day, and it changes each day as I go along.

FREDERICK BUECHNER

Faith and Fiction

Exactly a year ago tomorrow, the fifth of March, 1986, a very good friend of mine died. He was an Englishman—a witty, elegant, many-faceted man. One morning in his sixty-eighth year he simply didn't wake up. Which was about as easy a way as he could possibly have done it. But it wasn't easy for the people he left behind because it gave us no chance to say good-bye, either in words, if we turned out to be up to that, or in some unspoken way if we weren't. A couple of months later my wife and I were staying with his widow overnight in Charleston, South Carolina, when I had a short dream about him, which I want to tell you about.

I dreamed that he was standing there in the dark guest room, where my wife and I were asleep, looking very much the way he always did in the navy blue jersey and white slacks that he often wore, and I told him how much we missed him and how glad I was to see him again, and so on. He acknowledged that somehow. Then I said, "Are you really there, Dudley?" I meant was he there in fact and truth, or was I merely dreaming that he was? His answer was that he was really there. And then I said, "Can you prove it?" "Of course," he said. Then he plucked a strand of blue wool out of his jersey and tossed it to me, and I caught it between my index finger and my thumb, and the feel of it was so palpable and so real that it woke me up. That's all there was to the dream. But it was as if he had come on purpose to do what he had done and then left. When I told that dream at breakfast the next morning, I had hardly finished when my wife spoke. She said she had noticed the strand of wool on the carpet when she was getting dressed. She was sure it hadn't been there the night before. I thought I was losing my mind, and I rushed upstairs to see, and there it was—a little tangle of navy blue wool that I have in my wallet as I stand here today.

Another event was this. I went into a bar in an airport not long ago to fortify myself against my least favorite means of moving around the world. It was an off hour, so I was the only customer and had a choice of a whole row of empty barstools. And on the counter in front of each barstool there was a holder with a little card stuck in it, advertising the drink of the day, or something like that. I noticed that the one in front of me had an extra little bit of metal stuck on top of the card. It wasn't on any of the others, so I took a look at it. It turned out to be one of those tie clips that men used to wear. It had three letters engraved on it, and the letters were C. F. B. Those are my initials.

Lastly, this. I was receiving communion in an Episcopal church early one morning. The priest was an acquaintance of mine, and I could hear him moving along the rail from person to person as I knelt there waiting for my turn. The body of Christ, he said, the bread of heaven. The body of Christ, the bread of heaven. When he got to me he put in another word. The word was my name. "The body of Christ, Freddy, the bread of heaven."

The dream I had about my friend may very well have been just another dream, and you certainly don't have to invoke the supernatural to account for the thread on the carpet. The tie clip I find harder to explain away; it seems to me that the mathematical odds against its having not just one or two but all three of my initials and in the right order must be astronomical. But I suppose that too could be just a coincidence. On the other hand, in both cases there is also the other possibility. Far out or not, I don't see how any open-minded person can *a priori* deny it. And it's that other possibility that's at the heart of everything I want to say here on this Ash Wednesday night.

Maybe my friend really did come in my dream, and the thread was a sign to me that he had. Maybe it's true that by God's grace the dead are given back their lives and that the doctrine of the resurrection of the body is not just a doctrine. My friend couldn't have looked more substantial, less ectoplasmic, standing there in the dark, and it was such a crisp, no-nonsense exchange that we had. There was nothing surreal or wispy about it.

As to the tie clip, it seemed so extraordinary that for a moment I almost refused to believe that it had happened. Even though I had the thing right there in my hand, with my initials on it, my first inclination was to deny it—for the simple reason that it was so unsettling to my whole common-sense view of the way the world works that it was easier and less confusing just to shrug it off as a crazy fluke. We're all inclined to do that. But maybe it wasn't a fluke. Maybe it was a crazy little peek behind the curtain, a dim little whisper of providence from the wings. I had been expected, I was on schedule, I was taking the right journey at the right time. I was not alone.

What happened at the communion rail was different. There was nothing extraordinary about the priest knowing my name—I knew he knew it—and there was nothing extraordinary about his using it in the service because he evidently did that kind of thing quite often. But the effect on *me* was extraordinary. It caught me off guard. It moved me deeply. For the first time in my life, maybe, it struck me that when Jesus picked up the bread at his last meal and said, "This is my body which is for you," he was doing it not just in a ritual way for humankind in general, but in an unthinkably personal way for every particular man or woman or child who ever existed or someday would exist. Most unthinkable of all: maybe he was doing it for me. At that holiest of feasts we are known not just by our official name but by the names people use who have known us the longest and most intimately. We are welcomed not as the solid citizens that our Sunday best suggests we are, but in all our tackiness and tatteredness that nobody in the world knows better than each of us knows it about ourselves—the bitterness and the phoniness and the confusion and the irritability and the prurience and the half-heartedness. The bread of heaven, *Freddy*, of all people. Molly? Bill? Ridiculous little So-and-so? Boring old What's-his-name? Extraordinary. It seemed a revelation from on high. Was it?

Maybe all that's extraordinary about these three little events is the fuss I've made about them. Things like that happen every day to everybody. They're a dime a dozen; they mean absolutely nothing.

Or, things like that are momentary glimpses into a mystery of such depth, power and beauty that if we were to see it head on, in any way other than in glimpses, I suspect we would be annihilated. If I had to bet my life and my children's lives, my wife's life, on one possibility or the other, which one would I bet it on? If you had to bet your life, which would you bet it on? On "Yes, there is God in the highest," or, if that language is no longer viable, "There is mystery and meaning in the deepest"? Or on "No, there is whatever happens to happen, and it means whatever you choose it to mean, and that's all there is"?

Of course we can bet Yes this evening and No tomorrow morning. We may know we're betting; we may not know. We may bet one way with our lips, our minds, even our hearts, and another way with our feet. But we all of us bet, and it's our lives themselves we're betting with, in the sense that the betting is what shapes our lives. And of course we can never be sure we bet right because the evidence both ways is fragmentary, fragile, ambiguous. A coincidence, as somebody said, can be God's way of remaining anonymous, or it can be just a coincidence. Is the dream that brings healing and hope just a product of wishful thinking? Or is it a message maybe from another world? Whether we bet Yes or No is equally an act of faith.

There's a famous section in the Epistle to the Hebrews where the author, whoever it was, says that "faith is the substance of things hoped for, the evidence of things not seen." Marvelous definition. Noah, Abraham, Sarah, all the rest, it goes on to say, all died in faith, not having received what was promised but having seen it and greeted it from afar, and having acknowledged that they were strangers and pilgrims on the earth. For such people make it clear that they're seeking a homeland. Wonderful passage.

In other words, faith, it seems to me, is distinctly different from other aspects of religious life and not to be confused with them, even though we often use the word "faith" to mean religious belief in general, as in the phrase "What faith are you?" Faith is different from theology because theology is reasoned and systematic and orderly, whereas faith is disorderly and intermittent and full of surprises. Faith is different from mysticism because mystics in their ecstasy become one with what faith can at most see only from afar, as that passage from Hebrews says. Faith is different from ethics because ethics is primarily concerned not, like faith, with our relationship with God but with our relationship with each other. I think maybe faith is closest to worship because, like worship, it is essentially a response to God. It involves the emotions and the physical senses as well as the mind. But worship is consistent, structured, single-minded and seems to know what it's doing, while faith is a stranger, an exile on the earth, and doesn't know for certain about anything. Faith is homesickness. Faith is a lump in the throat. Faith is less a position *on* than a movement *toward*—less a sure thing than a hunch. Faith is waiting. Faith is journeying through space and time.

So if someone (and this frequently happens) were to come up and ask me to talk about my faith, it's exactly that journey through space and time I'd have to talk about. The ups and downs of the years, the dreams, the odd moment, the intuitions. I'd have to talk about the occasional sense I have that life isn't just a series of events causing other events as haphazardly as a break shot in pool causes billiard balls to go off in many different directions, but that life has a plot the way a novel has a plot—that events are somehow leading somewhere. Whatever your faith may be, or my faith may be, it seems to me inseparable from the story of what has happened to us. And that's why I believe that no literary form is better adapted to the subject of faith than the form of fiction.

Faith and fiction both journey forward in time and space and draw their life from that journey. They *are* that journey, really. They involve the concrete, the earthen, the particular, more than they do the abstract and the cerebral. In both faith and fiction the people you meet along the way, the things that happen to happen, the places— the airport bar, the room where you have a last supper with some friend—count for much more than ideas do. Fiction can hold opposites together in a story simultaneously, like love and hate, laughter and weeping, despair and hope, and so can faith, which by its very nature both sees and does not see. That's what faith is: seeing and not seeing, seeing dimly, seeing from afar. Probably its most characteristic utterance is that unforgettable one from the Gospel of Luke where a child is sick and Jesus says, "If you believe, I can heal him," and the man, speaking for everybody who has faith, says, "Lord, I believe; help thou my unbelief." Opposites.

Faith and fiction both start once upon a time and are continually changing and growing in mood and intensity and direction. When faith stops changing and growing, it dies on its feet. And, believe me, so does fiction when it stops growing and changing. And they have even more in common than that. They both start with a leap in the dark, to use that famous phrase. How can Noah or Abraham or Sarah or anyone else know for sure that the promise they die without receiving will be kept and that their journey in search of a homeland will ever get them home? How can anyone writing a novel or a story know for sure where it will lead and just how and with what effect it will end, or even if the story is worth telling? Let writers beware who from the start know too much about what they're doing and keep too heavy a hand on the reins. They leave too little room for luck, just as Abraham and Sarah, if they know too much about what they're doing as they live their stories, leave too little room for grace.

The word "fiction," as everybody in this room knows, comes from a Latin verb meaning to shape, to fashion, to feign. That's what fiction does, and in many ways it's what faith does, too. You fashion your story as you fashion your faith, out of the great hodgepodge of your life—the things that have happened to you and the things you've dreamed of happening. They're the raw material of both. Then, if you're a writer, like me, you try less to impose a shape on the hodgepodge than to see what shape emerges from it. You try to sense in what direction the hodgepodge of your life is moving. You listen to it. You avoid forcing your characters to march too steadily to the drumbeat of your artistic purpose. You leave some mea-sure of real freedom for your characters to be themselves. And if minor characters show an inclination to become major characters, as they're apt to do, you at least give them a shot at it, because in the world of fiction it may take many pages before you find out who the major char-acters really are, just as in the real world it may take you many years to find out that the stranger you talked to once for half an hour in the railway station may have done more to point you to where your true homeland lies than your priest or your best friend or even your psychiatrist.

Of course anybody who writes books uses as much craft as there is at hand. I certainly do that myself. I figure out what scenes to put in and—almost as hard—what scenes to leave out. I decide when to use dialogue and spend hours trying to make it sound like human beings talking to each other instead of like me talking to myself. I labor to find the right tone of voice, the right style, ultimately the right word to tell my story in, which is the hardest part, I suppose, of writing—sentence after sentence, page after page, looking for the word that has freshness and color and life.

I try not to let my own voice be the dominant one. It's hard to do that. The limitation of the great stylists—Henry James, say, or Hemingway—is that you remember their voices long after you've forgotten the voices of any of the people they wrote about. In one of the Psalms, God says, "Be still and know that I am God." I've always taken that to be good literary advice, too. Be still the way Tolstoy is still, be still the way Anthony Trollope is still, so that your characters can become gods and speak for themselves and come alive in their own way.

In both faith and fiction you *fashion* out of the raw stuff of your experience. If you want to remain open to luck and grace, you *shape* that stuff, less to impose a shape on it than to discover what the shape is. And in both, you *feign*. Feigning is imagining—making visible images for invisible things. Fiction has no way of being "true," the way a photograph is true; at its best it can only feign truth, the way a good portrait does, arriving at an inward, invisible truth. It can be true to the experience of being alive in the world, and what you write obviously depends on which part of your experience you choose to write about.

The part that has always most interested me is illustrated by incidents like the three I told you about at the start: the moment that unaccountably brings tears to your eyes, that takes you by crazy surprise, that sends a shiver down your spine, that haunts you with what is just possibly a glimpse of something far beyond or deep within itself. That's the part of human experience I choose to write about in my fiction. It's the part I'm most concerned to feign—that is, to make images for. In that sense I can live with the label of "religious novelist."

In any other sense I consider it the kiss of death. I lean over backward not to preach or to propagandize in my novels. I don't dream up plots and characters to illustrate some homiletic message. God forbid! I'm not bent on driving home some theological point. I'm simply trying to conjure up stories in which people are touched with what may or may not be the presence of God in their lives, the way I believe we all are as surely as I believe that I'm standing at this lectern, though most of us might sooner be shot dead than use that kind of language to describe it. In my own experience the ways God appears in our lives are elusive and ambiguous always. There's always room for doubt—in order, perhaps, that there will always be room to breathe. There's so much in life that hides God and denies the very possibility of God that sometimes it's hard not to deny God altogether. Yet it's still possible to have faith, in spite of all those things. Faith is that "in spite of." That's the experience I'm trying to be true to—in the same way that other novelists are trying to be true to the experience of being, say, a woman, or being an infantryman in the Second World War, or being black, or being whatever.

For all those novelists there is nothing more crucial than honesty. If you're going to be a religious novelist (and I'm not urging anybody) you've got to be honest not just about the times that glimmer with God's presence but also about the times that are dark with His absence because, needless to say, you've had your dark times just like everybody else.

Terrible things happen, for instance, in the four novels I wrote about a character named Leo Bebb. Bebb's wife, Lucille, kills her own baby. And when Bebb tells her long afterward that she has been washed clean with the Blood of the Lamb she says, "The only thing I've been washed in is the shit of the horse," and dies a suicide. Poor Brownie, another character, reeking of aftershave, decides that his rose-colored faith is as false as his teeth and loses his faith. Miriam Parr dies of cancer, wondering if she's "going someplace," as she puts it, or "just going out like a match."

The narrator of these four novels is a feckless young man named Antonio Parr, who starts out in the first book with no sense of commitment to anything or anybody, but who, through his relationship with Leo Bebb, gradually comes alive with at least the possibility of something like religious faith. He has learned to listen for God in the things that happen to him, just in case there happens to be a God to listen to. Maybe all he can hear, he says, quoting Andrew Marvell, is "time's winged chariot hurrying near." Or, if there's more to it than that, the most he can say of it constitutes the passage that ends the last of those four novels, where the narrator uses the Lone Ranger as an image for Christ and says:

> To be honest, I must say that on occasion I hear something else too—not the thundering of distant hooves, maybe, or "Hi-yo, Silver, away!" echoing across the lonely sage, but the faint chunk-chunk of my own moccasin heart, of the Tonto afoot in the dusk of me somewhere, who, not because he ought

to but because he can't help himself, whispers "kemo sabe" *every once in a while to what may or may not be only a silvery trick of the failing light.*

So terrible things as well as wonderful things happen in those novels. But it's not so much that I have to cook them up in order to give a balanced view of the way life is. It's that they have a way of happening as much on their own in the fictional world as they do in the real world. If you're preaching from a pulpit or otherwise grinding an ax, you only let the things happen that you want to have happen. But insofar as fiction, like faith, is a journey not only forward in space and time but a journey inward, it's full of surprises, the way dreams are. Even the wonderful things, the things that religious writers in the propagandist sense would presumably orchestrate and control, tend at their best to come as a surprise, and that's what's most wonderful about them. Again, in the case of the Bebb books, for instance, I was well along into the first of them, *Lion Country*, before I came to the conviction that Bebb himself was a saint. I hadn't known that. It was a marvelous surprise.

Imagine setting out *consciously* to write a novel about a saint. Think about that. How could a writer avoid falling flat on his face? Nothing is harder to make real than holiness. Certainly nothing is harder to make appealing and attractive. The danger is that you start out with the idea that sainthood is something people achieve—that you get to be holy more or less the way you get to be an Eagle Scout. To create a saint from that point of view would be to end up with something on the order of Little Nell. The truth, of course, is that holiness is not a human quality at all, like virtue. Holiness is Godness, and as such it's not something that people do, but something that God does in them.

It's something God seems especially apt to do to people who aren't virtuous at all, at least not to start with. Think of Francis of Assisi, or Mary Magdalene. If you're too virtuous, the chances are you think you're a saint already under your own steam, and therefore the real thing can't happen to you.

Leo Bebb, God knows, was not an Eagle Scout. He ran a religious diploma mill and ordained people through the mail for a fee. He did five years in the pen on a charge of indecent exposure involving children. He had a child with the wife of his twin brother. But he was a risk-taker. He was as round and fat and full of bounce as a rubber ball. He was without pretense. He was good company. Above all, he was extraordinarily alive—so much so for me, anyway, that when I was writing about him it was like a love affair. I couldn't wait to get to my study every morning. That's when I began not only to see that he was a saint but to see what a saint is.

A saint is a life-giver. I hadn't known that. A saint is a human being with the same hang-ups and dark secrets and abysses as the rest of us. But if a saint touches your life, you come alive in a new way. Even aimless, involuted Antonio Parr came more alive through knowing Bebb, though at first he was out to expose him as a fake. So did the theosophist Gertrude Conover, Bebb's blue-haired octogenarian paramour. More extraordinary yet, *I* came more alive. I'm a bookish, private sort of man, not given to standing up before as many people as you are in this room and making a fool of myself, but in my old age I find myself doing and saying all sorts of outrageous things which, before Bebb came into my life and into my fiction, I would never have even considered. I didn't think Bebb up at all, the way he finally emerged as a character; sometimes I wonder if he was the one who thought *me* up. I had an entirely different character in mind when I started. But in his tight-fitting raincoat and Tyrolean hat Bebb simply turned out to be the person he was in my journey of writing those books. I didn't expect him. I didn't deserve him. He came making no conditions; there were no strings attached. He was a gift to me.

And that's also (I want to be theological for a moment) what grace is. Grace is a gift, totally free. Grace is God in his givenness. "Inspiration" is the word that writers are apt to use for it—inspiration as a breathing into. In fiction, as in faith, something from outside ourselves is breathed into us if we're lucky and if we're open enough to inhale it. I think writers of religious fiction have to stay open in that way. They've got to play their hunches more and take risks more. They shouldn't try to keep too tight a rein on what they're doing. They should be willing to be less professional and less literary and to be more eccentric and more antic and more disheveled. Less like John Updike, let's say, or Walter Percy—very literary, very good— and more like Kurt Vonnegut or Peter DeVries or G. K. Chesterton.

In the stories of Flannery O'Connor, for instance, I have the feeling of the author herself being caught off guard by a flash of insight here, a stab of feeling there. She's making discoveries about holy things, about human things, in a way that she herself says would not have been possible if she had known too well where she was going and how she was going to get there. And as her readers we share in the freshness and the wonder of her surprise.

That greatest of all novels, *The Brothers Karamazov*, is a classic example of what I'm talking about—that great seething bouillabaisse of a book. It's digressive and sprawling, many too many characters in it, much too long, and yet it's a book which, just because Dostoyevsky leaves room in it for whatever comes up to enter, is entered here and there by maybe nothing less than the Holy Spirit itself, thereby becoming, as far as I'm concerned, what a religious novel at its best can be—that is, a novel less *about* the religious experience than a novel the reading of which is a religious experience: of God, both in his subterranean presence and in his appalling absence.

Is it the Holy Spirit? Is it the muse? Is it just a lucky break when these things happen in a story or in a life? Who dares say either way without crossing his fingers? But as in the journey of faith, it's possible every once in a while to be better than you are. Saint Paul says, "Do you not know that God's spirit dwells in you?" In the journey of fiction-making it's possible to write more than you know.

Bebb was a saint—a kind of saint, anyway—and when I finally finished with him, or he with me, I found it was very hard to write a novel about anybody who wasn't a saint. I tried to write a novel about a fifteenth-century alchemist. I tried to write a novel about a twentieth-century woman novelist. I tried to write a novel about a dishwasher in a restaurant in Manchester, Vermont. I tried to write one about an old lady in a nursing home. But one by one they all failed to come to life for me. They were all in their own way too much like me, I suppose, and after so many years I've become tired of me. And too many other authors were writing novels about people like that, many of them better than I could do it, so why add to the number? Then I realized that the reason why none of them worked for me was that, after

Bebb, only saints really interested me as a writer, and I've spent my life since then writing about them. There's so much life in them. They're so in touch with, so transparent to, the mystery of things that you never know what to expect from them. Anything is possible for a saint. They won't stay put or be led around by the nose, no matter how you try.

Then one day, entirely by accident, or by grace, or by luck, I came across a historical saint, named Godric, whom I'd never heard of before, who was born in England in 1065 and died there in 1170. If, like me, you don't happen to be a saint yourself, I don't know how you could possibly write about one without being given something from somewhere. That's especially true if you try, as I did, to make the saint himself your narrator, so that you have his whole interior life on your hands as well as his career. Add to that, Godric was a man who was born close to a thousand years ago. He lived in a different world, spoke a different language and saw things in a different way.

I did some research, needless to say—not the exhaustive kind that a real historical novelist does, because it wasn't primarily the history I was interested in, but Godric himself. Still, I did read enough to give myself a rough idea of what was going on in Europe at the time, especially in England. Largely through the ineffable *Dictionary of National Biography* I found out what I could about the historical figures who played some part in Godric's life, such as Abbot Ailred of Rievaulx Abbey and Ranulf Flambard, the Bishop of Durham and former chancellor to William II. I tried with very little success to find out what Rome and Jerusalem looked like when Godric made his pilgrimages there. And I dug a little into the First

Crusade because Godric was apparently involved with it briefly.

The principal source on Godric himself is a biography by someone who knew him, a monk known as Reginald of Durham, who also figures as a character in my novel. His book has never to this day been translated from medieval Latin into English. And in that connection something remarkable happened, comparable to my discovery of the tie clip with my initials on it. My own Latin came to an end when I was thirteen years old at the Lawrenceville School and had such a miserable time with Caesar's *Commentaries* that I gave it up forever. So the best I could do with this book in medieval Latin was to look up some promising items in the (happily) English index and then try to get the gist of the passages with the help of a dictionary. Just as I was getting started, struggling with this monstrous book, one of my daughters, who was off at boarding school, phoned to ask if she could bring some friends home for the weekend. And one of the friends turned out to be the chairman of the school's classics department—the only man, I suspect, within a radius of a million miles who could have done the job—and we sat together for a couple of hours two evenings in a row and he gave me sight translations of the passages I was after.

But I'm talking about something even odder than that, and a lot more precious. I'm talking about how, by something like grace, you're given every once in a while to be better than you are and to write more than you know. Not because of the research I did but in spite of it, Godric came alive for me. That's what I was given: the way he thought, the way he spoke, the humanness of him, the holiness of him. I don't think any writer can do that just by taking thought and effort and using the customary tools of the craft. Something else has to happen—something more mysterious. Godric not only came alive for me; he came speaking words that had a life and a twist to them that I can't feel entirely responsible for. I don't want to make it sound spookier than it was—I was the writer who wrote Godric's words; I dredged them up out of some subbasement of who I am. But the words that I found were much more like him than they were like me, and without him—whatever I mean by that—I feel certain that I never could have found them or written them.

Year after year, in the north of England, which I went to see again last year to remind myself of it, that old hermit Godric used to chasten his flesh in all seasons by bathing in the river Wear, which runs by Durham, at a place called Finchale. When he got too feeble to do that, to stagger down over the rocks and immerse his old carcass in that frigid water, he had a servant dig a hole in the chapel he had built for the Virgin Mary with his own hands out of wood (this is all from Reginald's life), and the servant would fill that hole up with water from the river so that Godric could still bathe in it. Here's a passage from my novel in which Godric describes what it was like to bathe first in the river itself and later in the little pool in the chapel:

First there's the fiery sting of cold that almost stops my breath, the aching torment in my limbs. I think I may go mad, my wits so outraged that they seek to flee my skull like rats on a ship that's going down. I puff. I gasp. Then inch by inch a blessed numbness comes. I have no legs, no arms. My very heart grows still. These floating hands are not my hands. This ancient flesh I wear is rags for all I feel of it.

"Praise, praise!" I croak. Praise God for all that's holy, cold and dark. Praise him for all we lose, for all the river of the years bears off. Praise him for

stillness in the wake of pain. Praise him for emptiness. And as you race to spill into the sea, praise him
yourself, old Wear. Praise him for dying and the
peace of death.

In the little church I built of wood for Mary, I
hollowed out a place for him. Perkin brings him by
the pail and pours him in. Now that I can hardly
walk, I crawl to meet him there. He takes me in his
chilly lap to wash me of my sins. Or I kneel down
beside him till within his depths I see a star.

Sometimes this star is still. Sometimes she dances.
She is Mary's star. Within that little pool of Wear she
winks at me. I wink at her. The secret that we share I
cannot tell in full. But this much I will tell. What's
lost is nothing to what's found, and all the death that
ever was, set next to life, would scarcely fill a cup.

Feigning is part of it. Imagining; image-making; reaching deep. But it feels like more than that, is what I'm
trying to say. Godric told me things I didn't know. He
revealed something of himself to me and something of
the distant past. He also revealed something of myself to
me and something of the not-so-distant future. Like Godric I'll grow old and I'll die. I think it was through his
eyes that I first saw beyond the inevitability of that to
the mercy of it. "All's lost. All's found." I have faith that
that is true, or someday will turn out to be true, but on
the old saint's lips the words have a ring of certitude and
benediction from which I draw courage, as I know I
couldn't draw courage from words merely of my own.

Is that why we write, year after year, people like me—
to keep our courage up? Are novels like mine a kind of
whistling in the dark? I think so. To whistle in the dark
is more than just to try to convince yourself that dark is

not all there is. It's also to *remind* yourself that dark is not all there is, or the end of all there is, because even in the dark there is hope. Even in the dark you have the power to whistle. And sometimes that seems more than just your own power because it's powerful enough to hold the dark back a little. The tunes you whistle in the dark are the images you make of that hope, that power. They are the books you write.

And in the same way, faith could also be called a kind of whistling in the dark. The living out of faith. The writing out of fiction. In both, you shape and you fashion and you feign. And maybe, finally, what the two have most richly in common is that they are a way of paying attention. Page by page, chapter by chapter, the story unfolds. Day by day, year by year, your own story unfolds—your life story. Things happen. People come and people go. The scene shifts. Time runs by. Time runs out.

Maybe it's all utterly meaningless. Maybe it's all unutterably meaningful. If you want to know which, pay attention to what it means to be truly human in a world that half the time we're in love with and half the time scares the hell out of us. Any fiction that helps us pay attention to that is religious fiction. The unexpected sound of your name on somebody's lips. The good dream. The strange coincidence. The moment that brings tears to your eyes. The person who brings life to your life. Even the smallest events hold the greatest clues. If it's God we're looking for, as I suspect we all are, maybe the reason we haven't found Him is that we're not looking very hard.

So pay attention. As a summation of all that I've ever had to say as a writer I'd settle for that. And as a talisman or motto for that journey in search of a homeland, which is what faith is, I'd settle for that, too.

HILLEL LEVINE

In Search of Sugihara

I wrote the book *In Search of Sugihara* because I was born to write that book. But it took me half a lifetime to discover that.

I think of myself as someone who was born when the ashes of Auschwitz were still warm. On the other hand, I grew up at a time in American life—and certainly in the history of its Jews—that was a golden age of security. The 1950s. I experienced my childhood as deceptively safe and stable, for there was a secret world that I knew about: the world of the death camps. It was almost a forbidden world, because there was so much denial on the part of my parents' generation—an eagerness to get beyond it.

Another event of my early childhood that had a major spiritual influence on me was the establishment of the state of Israel. Mine was not only the first generation of Jews to enjoy such security and opportunity; it was the first to witness the fulfillment of thousands of years of hope and prayer. Jews were returning to history. Jews now had the same problems that other people had: soldiers and police and border guards. But they also had the opportunity to exert their influence over major areas of society—not just to live their Jewishness in one corner of life, but to try to define what a Jewish society would be. That's been an important struggle for Israel, and it's been important for me to participate in it as a diaspora Jew who would like Israel to be a state that represents and embodies Jewish values, just as I want America to be the just and pluralistic society it can be.

As a teenager living in that golden age of security, however, I was only an observer, and that troubled me. All the major issues seemed to be happening somewhere else. I wanted to be active and responsible. The injunction from the Bible that spoke to me most strongly then, as it still does today, is the verse from Leviticus: "Do not stand on your neighbor's blood."

I was further torn between putting my body on the line—for civil rights, against further involvement in Vietnam, in support of a more vibrant America and a more vibrant Jewish community—and putting my body in the library, where I could develop the ideas and values that would enable me to take a more long-range view of all these issues. I was torn between the local and the global, the particular and the universal. I needed more inspiration and more facts.

So I became a wanderer at a young age. I created my own diaspora. When I was about sixteen, in the mid-1960s, I said good-bye to all that security and started traveling. I went to places that people in their "junior year abroad" don't go. I made a very solitary trip through Europe and the Soviet Union and its satellite countries, visiting the great cities and museums and treasures of

Western civilization and the graveyards of Jewish life. I met the "Jews of silence," the early Soviet Jewish dissidents whose heroic cries for truth and self-assertion weakened the Soviet Empire. I traveled as far as Ethiopia and lived in Ethiopian Jewish villages. The longing of those families for a lost Zion touched me deeply.

I shudder to think about who I was in those lonely quests, wandering through the geography of horror, looking for what I knew no longer existed. These are frightening things to do when you are so young. But it was clear to me that there were realities I had to discover, and that I had to learn how to harness their energy. There is some empowerment in standing on blood: power to observe, to feel, to analyze and to express.

One of my grandmothers left her home and her family in Eastern Europe at a young age. She came to America and lived here for the rest of her life. Twenty-five years later the mass murder began and she never saw her family again. The only thing she had left of her childhood was contained in a small brown paper bag. Sometimes she would take the bag out of a closet and show me an old Tsarist ruble, or an old photograph of a brother or a nephew or a niece, or the last letter she received from her family, in the early 1940s, telling her how bad things were getting. Those were the only artifacts she had left of her entire world. And I remember wondering: How can whole worlds be contained in one brown paper bag?

Trying to understand how that could be was what got me involved in the social sciences, in history and in Jewish history. I also became a rabbi. I studied at the Jewish Theological Seminary of America, in New York, partly because I was very young and couldn't commit myself to the doctor-lawyer-Indian chief career path, but also because I was very serious about study and about thinking of the meaning of life, and this seemed to be the best place to do both. I had wonderful mentors: men like Abraham Joshua Heschel and Elie Wiesel and Peter Berger, who combined the active and the contemplative life in ways that transformed me and gave me a model for expanding and enacting my concerns.

During those years as a student living on Morningside Heights, I often wandered through the streets of Harlem. One day, on West 123rd Street, near Fifth Avenue, I discovered a black-Jewish synagogue. Just what the connection of Rabbi Matthews and his followers was to historical Judaism wasn't clear to me. But that soon became unimportant. For four years I attended services at that synagogue on almost every Sabbath and took part in the life of the community. It was a place where I could experience the divine presence and also contribute to the civil rights movement from safer and slightly more familiar turf.

I had no interest in becoming a professional rabbi. Instead I chose another pulpit—I became a professor of sociology, trying to combine the richness of historical detail with disciplined thinking about how to observe and to analyze. Teaching suited me, and when I went to Yale in the 1970s I became engaged in university life far more deeply than I had ever been engaged as a student in my own college days.

But I soon realized with a shock that there was a contradiction in my teaching. I was trying to give my students intellectual tools with which to understand complex social relations and historical events. But when they repeated what they had learned it seemed so deterministic, almost mechanistic. I saw that my teaching, instead of developing their sense of individual responsibility, was doing just the opposite, and that I had to change the way I taught.

I would have to mount an attack on "no-fault" history, emphasizing that to explain behavior is not to excuse it— that people are ultimately responsible for their actions, even if their choices are limited and they are governed by social forces that they poorly understand. I needed to start teaching out of what I believed, not only out of what I had studied.

My concern for human freedom is nurtured by my religious beliefs and commitments. I believe that whatever God there may be is a God that is all-powerful and all-good. For a Jew of my generation, of course, that's a contradiction of cosmic proportions, the kind that theologians have wrestled with in every generation. My response is not that God has retired to Miami Beach, or that God neglects the world, or that God has become impotent in old age. My response is that God, as a very precious gift, gives people freedom, gives people commandments, gives people a sense of right and wrong, gives people a passion for life, all of which can be distorted or perverted, but nevertheless people are given freedom. People are free to create the Auschwitzes. People are free to create the Beethoven symphonies. People are even free, like the German conductor Wilhelm Furtwängler and his musicians, to give magnificent performances of Beethoven's Ninth Symphony, with its heart-stirring affirmations of the familial connections between men and women, while their people were killing millions of my people. We have to understand those moments and those contradictions. That's the raw material.

One of the courses I taught during my university years, first at Yale and later at Boston University, was called "the sociology of evil." Hundreds of students signed up; it became almost a cult course. Usually the social sciences don't talk about evil; they try to tame it by using clinical categories like "deviance." So my course was partly a critique of those disciplines. But it was also a rehearsal. I felt that I just wasn't ready yet to teach the Holocaust itself; I was afraid that somehow it would be trivialized, that I wouldn't get it right.

Then, in the late 1980s, a project came along that would help me to break through my fears and get beyond the mystery of evil to the Holocaust itself. With the investigative journalist Larry Harmon I wrote a book called *The Death of an American Jewish Community*, about how American bankers and bureaucrats incited conflicts between blacks and Jews in changing neighborhoods. Doing the research for that book enabled me to consider the different combinations of venality and stupidity that go into large-scale destructiveness, even when the efforts are honorably motivated, as we implied in the book's subtitle, "a tragedy of good intentions."

That book changed me as a writer. Larry taught me to write clearly and also, probably, to think clearly. But what was best about the experience was that we got the people to talk about their lives. The book could have been presented with tables and charts; we were dealing really with who gets mortgages, and at what rates, and under what conditions. Instead we interviewed the men and women in the neighborhood and had them tell us their story. Suddenly I realized that I love asking people about themselves and trying to figure out how they fit into God's world. I also remembered how important Jewish stories have always been to me in my work.

As it turned out, it was the story of one man, Chiune Sugihara, a Japanese diplomat in Lithuania on the eve of World War II who saved as many as ten thousand Jews by giving them exit visas, that would take over my life and my energies and my emotions for most of the 1990s.

With that story, which became my book *In Search of Su-gihara*, you might say I went from the evil business to the goodness business.

In Search of Sugihara developed out of depression—deep depression. In the early 1990s the hope for a peaceful world resulting from the end of the Cold War had in fact degenerated into a new barbarism in the former Yugoslavia and elsewhere. I found myself thinking back to 1989, when I spent a semester in China on a State Department faculty exchange program. Living in a country that I knew so little about was an experience of radical otherness. In this case, unlike those solitary trips I had made several decades earlier, I was not alone. I was able to share the experience with my wife and my three children, and it was wonderful.

Those were great days in the People's Republic—there was liberalization and a sense of optimism—and I walked with my children around Tiananmen Square and told them about how fearful we used to be of China and the other communist countries. I told them about the air-raid drills we had when I was growing up in the 1950s: what it was like in school when you heard a siren and had to climb under the desk to protect yourself from the bombs that these people, these wonderful soldiers strolling through Tiananmen Square, were going to drop on us. And how absurd that fear was—you know, people are people. Yet only a few weeks later those same soldiers were driving tanks through lines of student protesters. In that very square where I was telling my children about our false fears, there were now pools of blood. That shook my sense of being able to predict anything about the future and to give a reasonable assessment of the past. We thought things were getting better.

73

Similarly, while it's certainly a blessing that the Soviet Union collapsed, who could have predicted the acts of brutality and "ethnic cleansing" that followed the breakdown of communism, especially in Yugoslavia, or the massacres that have been committed in Rwanda and many other countries, all of which were greeted with passive acceptance by the western world. Even the Holocaust, it seemed, hadn't pushed the outer limits of violence that people can perpetrate on each other. That's what I found so depressing. I was depressed by my inability to do anything. I thought my life work was to do everything possible to make sure nothing like the Holocaust could ever happen again.

Finally I just couldn't stand being an unengaged observer any longer. I had to go to Yugoslavia and see the situation for myself. I called my local newspaper and asked for press credentials. I called a friend who worked for a human rights organization and borrowed a bulletproof vest, and I was off. My plan was to head for Sarajevo. As I was leaving the house my children grabbed me and asked me to promise that I wouldn't go to Sarajevo, that it was too dangerous. I didn't know what to say, because I really wanted to go to Sarajevo. On the other hand, I didn't want to get killed; my children had a point. Should I promise them and cross my fingers? How does one handle a conflict like that?

In the end I decided to keep my word to my children. I spent two weeks in Croatia observing the battlegrounds and interviewing refugees on all sides. I saw deeply disturbing things there and heard horrendous stories. One story that was typical of so much that I heard was told to me by a Bosnian woman who lived in a town called Pakrac: how in the morning we drank coffee with our neighbors and in the afternoon they came back and hacked us to pieces. How do neighbors hack each other to pieces? All my insights into human behavior and social organization were worthless. I had no way of explaining this behavior, and I came back home, intellectually and spiritually shaken.

Life has its own rhythms—and mysteries. A few days later I flew to Lithuania to give the inaugural lecture for the first university program in Judaic studies to be established in the former Soviet Union, in Vilnius. The timing was ironic. At Pakrac I had just seen the grim consequences of the decline of that evil empire. Yet here I was bound for Lithuania to celebrate the rebirth of Jewish life on former Russian soil. Historically, Vilnius, which the Jews called Vilna, "the Jerusalem of Lithuania," was a great intellectual center of world Jewry. So many of the movements that shaped centuries of Jewish life and that had a major influence on my own life developed there.

But when I got to the university and gave my lecture it was as if I understood the Holocaust for the first time, even after all those solitary pilgrimages and all those years of teaching. As I stood at the podium and looked out over the audience, I realized that I was dedicating this center for Judaic studies in the presence of the last surviving Jews of old Vilna; there were only five in the audience. It was an encounter with nothingness.

My Lithuanian hosts were very obliging. Afterward, they wanted me to enjoy the beauties of their country, and they suggested that we go sightseeing. Where does one go sightseeing in Lithuania? To the killing fields. So they took me to Ponar, where a large number of Jews were thrown in a ditch and shot by Nazi soldiers. A coldness and a depression that I had never experienced before overtook me.

Suddenly I happened to remember the story of Sugihara, which I had heard from a religious leader in Kyoto on one of my trips to Asia and had filed in my long-term memory. Now it came rushing back. I realized that Kovno, where Sugihara issued all those visas that saved all those Jews, was only a few hours' drive away. I had to see that consulate building, and I asked my hosts to take me there. They said, "There's nothing to see—it's just an apartment house. Let's go to some other massacre site." I said, "No, no, I want to see where this happened."

So they drove me to Kovno, and with the help of a local Jew we found the building on a small street, a few blocks from the center of town. I recognized the stucco facade and the curved staircase from having once seen a photograph of the building. And as I stood there I pictured Sugihara standing on the balcony looking out at the crowds of Jews who were lining up in front of embassies and consulates all over Europe in 1939. And I saw Sugihara, not doing what other diplomats were doing—closing their doors, closing their hearts—but issuing visas as fast as he could write them. I saw Sugihara's hand, signing the visas. And then I saw the hand of Josef Mengele, choosing the Jews he wanted for his unspeakable medical experiments at Auschwitz. Sugihara and Mengele, with the same hand. I thought of the powers that God endows us with for good or bad, to help others or to destroy them.

I was transfixed. The day was bitterly cold—well below zero—but I couldn't move. My hosts got very impatient: why was I just standing there? But I literally couldn't move, for a long time. At that moment I knew that I had to understand the hand of Sugihara. What made this man tick?

When I got back home to Boston, in my usual cautious

way I did a literature search. I went to the library and looked up "good." If my professional life was about to turn in a new direction I would have to educate myself on the subject. However, I found very little on goodness. I found many books on mass murderers—the gunmen who go into playgrounds and shoot children—but there was almost nothing on mass rescuers. I didn't understand why that should be. There was some great mystery there—the mystery of goodness, as compelling as the mystery of evil. I decided to try to unravel it.

And as I set out, my depression lifted. At last I was embarked on a positive journey. Because I had given a few lectures in Japan I knew some people there whom I could ask for help, and I began by getting in touch with them. They told me that Sugihara died in 1986; I had missed him by only a few years. But his wife and his family were still alive—there had been a few newspaper articles about them. Meanwhile, I also turned up the names of some of the people Sugihara had rescued. They were scattered in many parts of the world, and I flew to those places and tracked them down.

The portrait of Sugihara that began to emerge from my interviews was of a civil servant who inexplicably stretched the rules and took huge risks. He issued transit visas to anyone who applied, whatever documents they presented or whatever explanation they gave for not having the right documents, or any documents. The more visas Sugihara issued, the more Jews lined up at the consulate, and when his hand got tired from all that writing and signing he authorized his assistants to use rubber stamps. He kept the consulate open longer than he should have, and even when he and his family were ordered to leave Kovno he continued to issue visas from the window of his moving train.

But as the survivors talked to me I realized that they

had coated the story in terms that were almost impersonal. Their rescue was still so incredible to them, half a century later, that they couldn't think of Sugihara as a real person. They didn't even know his name; they thought of him as an angel, and they called him by that word: the *malakh*. The more I delved into the story, the more it just didn't add up. My instinct as a historian was that I should check the archives in Japan to see whether any documents existed.

So I flew to Tokyo in the summer of 1993 and just presented myself at the archives. I was able to get in and was well received. There were no folders on Sugihara. By then, however, I knew enough about him to ask the right questions to get other folders. On my first day I found a list of 2,139 names of people Sugihara had helped to escape, which he sent to his superiors in Tokyo. Later I realized that many of these were heads of households. Extrapolating from that list and from other files, we can estimate the number of people he rescued at close to ten thousand.

The standard story that had been told by his second wife and many other people was that Sugihara was a diplomat who was sent to Lithuania; that he asked permission from the Foreign Office in Tokyo to help the Jews and was denied; that he asked a second time and was told, "Absolutely not—it will complicate our relationships with our ally, Nazi Germany"; that he asked a third time and received a response of icy silence, whereupon he proceeded to issue the visas anyway, and that when he went home after the war he was fired for his disobedience and deprived of his pension and humiliated.

But that story was full of holes. For one thing, I didn't understand why the Japanese would suddenly send a diplomat to Lithuania in 1939 to open a consulate; Lithuania was a backwater, and the Japanese had never had a consulate there before. And why Sugihara? At the archives in Tokyo I found a record of his having told his superiors exactly what he was doing—an extensive correspondence in which he kept his bosses fully informed—and there were *no* return letters telling him "Don't do it." I also discovered that it was Japanese policy at that time to authorize their diplomats to issue transit visas to anyone who had a destination and enough money to cover expenses during a short stopover in Japan.

Now the standard version *really* didn't make sense. I realized that hundreds of documents existed and that I would never get anywhere sitting at a desk with only one translator. On the other hand, those were the days when the yen was the yen; I had about $2,000, and translators cost $1,000 a day. So there was no chance of professionalizing my research unless I went back to the United States and applied for research grants. I had tried that once, but I didn't succeed because I wasn't a Japanese scholar. Research grants are only given to people in the field, and this wasn't my field.

Fortunately, I had done some teaching in Tokyo in the 1980s, and I found some former students who were willing to work for me at McDonald's-type summer wages. Then word got out, and I began to get telephone calls from wives of Japanese diplomats and other foreign ministry people, mostly women. Those women were extremely intelligent. They weren't trained as historians, but they had lived abroad for many years and spoke excellent English, and they volunteered to help me. Pretty soon I had a whole cottage industry at work in the archives. The foreign ministry had never seen anything like it. Ordinarily, Japanese historians come in and ask for a document and say "Thank you" and walk out. The people in the ministry said, "You've been camping out here for two months." It ended up being the best graduate seminar I ever had.

Later I took that research and followed the trail to many other countries. I located Sugihara's first wife in a nursing home in Australia. She was ninety-three years old, and when I interviewed her she confirmed my sense that Sugihara was a good man. Two days later she died. It was as if she had been waiting for me all those years.

Altogether it was a great journey of discovery, finding so many sources that reflected on this mysterious man and the banality of his goodness. It turned out that Sugihara wasn't a diplomat, but a spy—a major spy, representing the Japanese pro-Nazi faction in Europe, trying to find out what the Nazis were really doing and how that should affect the alliance that the Japanese were contemplating. Meanwhile he was also working for the Nazis, gathering information for them, as I discovered in the Nazi archives in Freiburg. It was all there. I also found his paper trail in the Soviet archives in Moscow and even in our National Archives in Washington.

Yet at a certain point this man looked at the crowds of Jewish men and women and children who lined up outside his consulate in Kovno every day and felt that he just couldn't let them be killed. He knew better than they what fate awaited them, and he took enormous risks to save them. Not only did he issue all those transit visas to Japan; he persuaded diplomats and officials in other nations to authorize the passage of those Jewish refugees through their own countries. The result was one of the largest mass rescues in World War II.

Why did he do it? I'm still learning. I still don't know.

But I do know that my search was worth all the miles that went into it. I searched for a hero and found that what was heroic about Sugihara was his ordinariness. Everything about his long life was ordinary except for a few months in the summer of 1940. His story tells me that ordinary people can rise to extraordinary acts and can precipitate extraordinary acts in other people.

I see Sugihara at the center of a conspiracy of goodness. If he had only issued Japanese visas, without also securing the escape route to his own country, half a world away, not a single Jew would have been saved. But the power of his moral leadership was so great that he was able to evoke goodness in other people. He thereby mysteriously enlisted those people in his conspiracy to prevent life from being wasted.

For me his example extends the boundaries of human possibility. Who knows? If there had been a thousand Sugiharas, or a hundred, or even only ten, perhaps there would not have been a Holocaust.

DAVID BRADLEY

Bringing Down the Fire

I'm bad at titles. I usually let other people make them up for me. Which is what I did with this talk: "Bringing Down the Fire" is stolen from the text of a science fiction novel that I found in the stacks of the Bedford County Public Library, in Pennsylvania, in 1965 when I was fifteen years old.

There's a lot that I don't recall about that book—like the name of the author, the name of the hero, and, in fact, the name of the book. What I do recall is the basic situation. It was a science fiction novel about the aliens— one of those non-human races who have names that are all consonants. They had landed on Earth and they had the situation well in hand. Humankind seemed to have adjusted well to virtual slavery and even, as I recall it, to cannibalism. Everybody was hustling around like cab drivers trying to please the aliens so as to stay out of the stew pot. To keep it that way, the aliens promoted a religion of acceptance, which was run by a human priesthood.

But what the aliens didn't know was that the priesthood had an inner cabal dedicated to reclaiming Earth and destroying the aliens. These priests were unarmed, but they had developed a mental potential to an incredible degree. Their memories were huge; they had this computerized mental process—telepathy and telekinesis and teleportation—and one awesome weapon that they called bringing down the fire out of heaven. What that was was to reach with the mind into the heart of a star and pull the plasma out and down onto the surface of a planet. They didn't practice on Earth, since the process obviously did nothing good to the planet. In fact, they didn't practice at all. The good news was that you could learn to bring down fire. The bad news was that you had to be down there on the planet to do it. So if you were successful the process did nothing good to you, either.

The prologue of the book was a prophesy that someone would appear who could not only bring the fire out of heaven but live to tell the tale. And the hero, of course, was just such a person, a young man who was completing his training as a priest but who had, known only to himself, mastered something that the order did not teach— the ability to separate his mind into two parts, to mentally be in two places at once. This allowed him both to stand on the ground while he was bringing down the fire and to float above the ground and possibly save himself from the fire he was bringing down in his own head.

Which is exactly what he did. He was hovering in space above a barren airless planet, watching himself below bringing the fire out of the heart of the sun. The odd thing was that he did it in the beginning of the book. Right up front. Chapter one. You'd think that would have ended things: "O.K., now that we can do this, let's go Rambo the aliens." The writer of that novel knew better, which is probably why I remember as much of it as I do.

In some ways that book made little impression on me. For example, the rest of the plot escapes me, although I think I can figure it out now. The young man would have to learn that there's more to liberation than a bunch of pyrotechnics; you can't liberate people who don't want to go. But otherwise that book made a tremendous impression on me—so much so that when I began to think about my talk here tonight, that image of a young man floating in space and bringing down the fire sprang into my mind. This time I knew what the hero of that novel was doing in a way I certainly didn't know when I first read the book.

I come from a long line of preachers, beginning with a gentleman named Peter Bradley, a freed slave from Delaware, who in the early part of the nineteenth century was licensed to preach in the African Methodist Episcopal Zion Church, one of several denominations formed at about that time by blacks who objected to the segregation they were subjected to in the regular Methodist Church. A lot of people have this weird notion about the black church. There ain't no "the black church." There are many black churches. Jesse Jackson, for instance, is not a Methodist. If Jesse Jackson were a Methodist he'd have a bishop to tell him to go home. Only Baptists get to tip around the country as long as their congregations will put up with it.

My tradition is Methodist, and in the Methodist religion you do what you're told. Peter Bradley's son was Daniel Francis Bradley. He followed in his father's footsteps as a preacher and took the additional step of becoming a presiding elder. Those of you who know these organized denominations know that the presiding elder is an official who rides around and supervises several ministers in a given geographical area. Daniel Francis Bradley's district was an area of western Pennsylvania and Ohio, and in 1910 he settled his family in a small Pennsylvania town called Bedford. My father was then about five years old. His name was David Henry Bradley, and he followed in his father's footsteps, first as a preacher and later as a presiding elder. He also became a general officer of the church with nationwide responsibilities—particularly, to travel around running Christian education conferences.

He also had an odd hobby. The local Bedford church was really too small to support a minister, so for twenty years my father acted as its pastor. As a result, I "grew up in the church," as they say—not so much in a religious sense, but in the sense that I had the opportunities for leadership experience that the black church has traditionally offered. First I was an usher; then I graduated to the choir, and taught Sunday school, and led the worship service on Sundays when my father was out of town.

I should say that I was not a very good preacher. I upset the ladies and gentlemen of the church—there were about fifteen of them—by seeking out obscure Scripture lessons in the apocryphal books of the Bible and by analyzing the implications of the hymns we were singing. If you want to screw up a bunch of Christians, analyze their hymns. Once I even drew a Scripture lesson from the Koran, though I had enough sense not to tell them what I was doing. I learned the hard way that I wasn't much of a preacher. I had already come to the conclusion I wasn't much of a Christian—a fact which, in the years that followed, became obvious to all of us, so much so that my father never once suggested that I follow in the family business. In fact, he seemed mightily relieved that I never said I wanted to be a preacher.

My real experience with religion, however, didn't take place in Bedford but in the South. I've written about that, so I'd like to read one passage in which I tried to describe what that experience was like:

When I was four or five, my father started taking me with him on some of his travels, usually in the summer, when his work took him mostly to the Southeast. The first place I went with him—and it became a regular trip—was Dinwiddie, Virginia, where, in an aging ramshackle three-story building, the church operated an "Institute"—a combination Christian education workshop, summer camp and revival meeting.

The Institute ran for three weeks. The format was a day of classes punctuated by morning and noon chapel services, an afternoon recreation period, and three meals of good plain food, climaxed by the evening worship. The morning and afternoon worship services were short and pretty plain affairs. The evening service was pageantry, if for no other reason than that it was the focal point of everybody's day. To the "young people" worship was important because it was the closest they could get to a dating situation, and they made the most of it. They used to put their arms around each other and say, "Let's go to church." It was important to the ministers, who shared the various offices of the church and of the church service on a rotating basis, competing eagerly for the choice assignments, preaching and praying. It was important to the people in the community, who used the evening worship as a kind of camp meeting. And it was important to me because the Institute was not equipped with a radio or a TV, and worse, had a limited number of books; I was so desperate for reading matter that I practically memorized the begats.

Evening worship began with the arrival of the audience, the scrubbed youths and their chaperones, followed closely by the people from the community: the older ladies in out-of-fashion but immaculate dresses and toilet water; the men, seeming all of an age, with big rough hands poking out of the cuffs of suit coats worn awkwardly; the younger girls, in light dresses, casting flirtatious glances at the young men of the Institute (who were usually from cities and therefore sophisticated) and sharp challenging looks at the Institute's young women (who were also usually from the city and therefore seen as probably a little wild). They would all troop into the dilapidated auditorium, filling the rows of ragtag seating— trestle benches, tip-up seats from abandoned theaters, folding chairs mended with cardboard, even a couple of mismatched church pews—and wait impatiently for the ministers.

The ministers entered from the front, moving more or less in time to the sound that came from an off-key beaten-up piano. They were not unfamiliar figures—they were around all day, teaching classes, arguing points of theology and church politics, and playing Chinese checkers beneath the trees. Now they were solemn and dignified in black suits and clerical collars, each intent on performing his role, no matter how minor, with as much style as he could muster.

Performance was the word, for the service was high drama, from the solemnly intoned ritual invocation to the rolling hymns sung by a hundred people who needed no hymnals, in passionate voices that overpowered the doubtful leadership of the gap-toothed piano, to the hucksterish importunings over the collection plate, as a minister would announce the total and then proceed to cajole, shame or bully the audience into bringing it higher. There was no applause, of course, but the performance of each minister was rewarded with responses from the worshipers, the preaching and the praying being applauded with spontaneous choruses of "Amen, Amen," "Yes, Yes, Yes," and the ultimate accolade, "Preach on! Preach on!" Which they did, sometimes until midnight.

But the real ultimate accolade of a sermon was not even those shouts from the amen corner. It was when the doors of the church were opened and the call was sent out to those who wished to come to a makeshift altar and commune with God. I used to sit and watch the people as they decided. First there would be a little hesitation. And gradually people would begin to go up. They would leave their seats and go up and kneel to dedicate and rededicate themselves to Jesus. I used to see a little light in their eyes, glow in their face, redness, heat. I never answered that call to the altar myself; my father didn't approve of such displays. It's really not a Methodist thing, you know, to have a public display of anything. And of course there were political implications of a preacher's son taking such an action. People might say, "Well, what were you before if you just joining up now?"

But the real reason I never went up was that I didn't

91

feel what they felt. I wanted to go, but I didn't have the emotion that would make it legitimate. That's not to say that I didn't believe there was a mystery; I believed that there was some special communication that took place between that minister and those people. And I believed that it went on at the altar when they got closer to the preacher, because I saw the light in their eyes when they went up, and I admired them for it. But I saw the light in their eyes when they came back, and it was brighter. And I envied it. I felt embarrassed and inadequate that the fire had never touched me. In my heart I suspected it was because I was unworthy.

I was at last touched by the fire when I was eighteen. The year was 1968 and the place was Philadelphia. And it wasn't a church sanctuary but a classroom at the University of Pennsylvania, where I was a freshman. The Scripture lesson was taken from the Second Book of Samuel, the 13th through the 18th chapters; especially Samuel 15, verses 19 through 22, and Samuel 18, verse 33. The minister was a Southerner, but he wasn't a passionate black man at all; rather, he was a distinguished looking white-haired, white-skinned gentleman, a descendant of a Confederate Civil War colonel and a self-styled rum smuggler, a sometime drunk and a fairly blatant racist.

I'm not going to tell you all that went on as I read William Faulkner's *Absalom, Absalom*. But I'll summarize by saying this: it was the first book I ever really read. Of course I had read lots of books, but I had read them as I'm afraid most people do these days. I'd start out on the first page and end on the last page, and maybe I thought about it a little bit. But then I sort of put it down, because I had done it—I assumed that the thing was an experience when it was experienced. The truth was, I didn't know how to read.

But *Absalom, Absalom* was a book that I read. I had to read and reread it because the first time I didn't understand it; there were different versions of the same story, so I had to go back and reread just to figure out what happened. And, of course, on the second reading I had figured out that I couldn't figure out what had happened, because each version was told not only from a different point of view but from a biased point of view. And then I had to think about all that, which meant that I had to think about what the story meant. And then I had to read it again to develop some arguments about the racial aspect of the thing. Because this was, after all, the late sixties, and everything, including books written in the thirties, was being judged as much on political as on esthetic grounds, and in a great many circles, some of which included me, literary criticism had degenerated into *ad hominem* argument. One night in the library a young black woman saw what I was reading and said, "How can you deal with that shit? The man was a racist." Which was an accusation that gave me pause for more reasons than one.

The net result of all that activity was that I spent the better part of three months living with the book—reading it, and reading all about it, and searching the Bible for references, and searching through Faulkner's statements on race and statements about those statements, and trying to understand how it was that a man who probably wouldn't have wanted to touch me had been able to touch me so firmly. And somewhere in there—it took me till maybe my sixth or seventh reading, not because there was anything wrong with the book but because I just really didn't know how to read and I was a tight-assed little intellectual to boot—I underwent a religious conversion.

I wasn't entirely crazy here. I had been "carefully taught" to respond religiously to a book like *Absalom,*

Absalom once I saw what it was, which was basically a set of gospels about the life of a mythic figure named Thomas Sutpen, much as the New Testament is a set of gospels about the life of Christ. It was told in rich, figurative language full of symbolism and hooked firmly into what Jung called the archetype of the collective unconscious. In fact, it's possible that the only way I knew how to respond to *Absalom, Absalom* was religiously.

William James, in *The Varieties of Religious Experience*, described his experience of a man named Stephen Bradley (no relation of mine, by the way). In James's account, Bradley says: "Many of the young converts would come to me and ask if I had religion. And my reply generally was, 'I hope I have.' This did not appear to satisfy them. They said they knew *they* had it. I requested them to pray for me. Thinking that if I had not got religion now, after so long a time professing to be a Christian, it was time I had."

In 1829, James continues, Stephen Bradley attended a Methodist worship service "in which there was good preaching, but which left my feelings still unmoved." But later that night the holy spirit visited Stephen Bradley:

"At first I began to feel my heart beat very quick, all of a sudden, which made me at first think that perhaps something is going to ail me. Though I was not alarmed, for I felt no pain. My heart increased its beating. I began to feel exceedingly happy and humble. Such a sense of unworthiness as I had never felt before. In the meantime, amid all this exercise, a thought rose in my mind: 'What can it mean?' Now all at once, as if to answer it, it appeared to me, as if some candle lighted." And that lighted candle compelled Bradley to witness: "After breakfast I

went round to converse with my neighbors on religion, which I could not have been hired to do before
this. And at their request I prayed with them in public, though I had never prayed in public before."

Now I knew nothing of Stephen Bradley, or William
James, or archetypes, or anything else when I was sitting
in the Van Pelt Library at the University of Pennsylvania
reading *Absalom, Absalom* for the umpteenth time. But I
felt those things. My heart beat and something came on
in my mind. And I did feel unworthy. However, I also
felt a certain sense of dedication. I envied William Faulkner. But I also knew what I wanted to do with the rest
of my life.

I was prepared to do that, I suppose, by my lineage
and to some extent by the church's order of service,
which is a template for dramatic experience. But in the
final analysis I didn't really understand what I had taken
on because I still didn't understand how William Faulkner could feel as he did and write as he did and affect
me as he did. That would come later.

"Later" began to happen in 1977 when I accepted an
assignment from a travel magazine to write an article
about the island of Haiti. I was lucky to get it; I wasn't
very experienced—I had only done two other magazine
articles. Actually I'd had several assignments but I had
screwed them up. In fact, the reason I got the assignment
was because I was not experienced. The editor said he
wanted a travel article that didn't look like a travel article,
and since I didn't know how to write one anyway . . . The
simple fact was that he couldn't find anybody else who
was willing to go tipping off to Haiti, which was the land
of voodoo religion. To a travel editor that seemed roman-

tic. But it was also the land of Baby Doc Duvalier and the Tontons Macoute, and that's not romantic in the least.

I found my way into that article through an exhibition at the Brooklyn Museum on Haitian art—those bright, vibrant paintings produced by artists who are called "primitive" because they weren't formally trained but which nevertheless seem to capture all the emotional heat and raw energy of the tropical sun. What else they captured was something I discovered when I reached the island and began to understand how that art was produced. There were old masters in Haiti. Well, they weren't all that old, since to the rest of the world Haitian art began during World War II. In any case, some of those artists were still alive. And they weren't really untrained primitives, either. Nearly all of them were voodoo priests, or *houngan*. And they were trained by religion, voodoo, in which the act of invocation, the bringing of the spirit of the gods, or *loa*, begins with the drawing of a complex and precise spirit map called a *vèvè*. These intricate patterns are incorporated into some of the most powerful of the paintings. In Haiti you don't have to be a preacher to be an artist. But you *do* have to be an artist to be a preacher, because if you screw up the *vèvè* the best thing that can happen is that the gods don't come. The worst thing that can happen is that they come and they're pissed off.

There's also a new generation of artists in Haiti, or was in 1977—they may have all been shot by now. Unlike the "primitives," they were formally trained. And they were no longer primarily voodoo priests, or at least they weren't admitting it, which was a good idea since the government had declared that voodoo no longer existed. But they were still drawing on voodoo themes, still incorporating the intricate patterns and exploring them and developing them into new images.

There were other artists, however, who worked in sweatshops, paid by what they call art galleries in Haiti to produce pieces that look just like the art of the old masters. The stuff sells like hotcakes to tourists from France and America. It's ugly as sin—in fact, the new generation of real artists call it "neon-primitive." Some of it actually glows. Day-Glo on velvet.

Well, I wanted to write about all that. And I did try to write, in words that I think apply not only to the visual arts but to other artistic endeavors that I now realize were closer to my heart than I might have known at the time—certainly closer than I would be willing to admit. I posed a question to one of the new artists, a man named Jacques Gabriel, about why there was so much "neon-primitive" art. One reason, of course, was that the tourists bought it—the law of supply and demand. But there was another economic law to be considered—Gresham's Law, which says that bad money drives out good money. Wouldn't bad art drive out good art? Wouldn't the real work of the new generation be lost in the neon glare of all that handicraft?

What "real" means when one is talking of art is, of course, an eternal debate. But surely all sides of that debate could agree that part of what it means is that somewhere, if only in the depths of the heart and the private dark of the night, the artist believes in what he or she is doing, believes that there is something inside him or her—knowledge of culture, emotion, personal anguish—that finds expression in the content or the style.

But how could young and unknown artists, talented but broke, in a country where starvation is a common way of death, do the real thing when it was so easy, so lucrative, and in some ways so necessary for survival to offer what was imitation? Especially when recognition seemed so hard to come by, when most of those in the outside world who spoke of Haitian art seemed to prefer not to recognize the new artists as even existing, not to admit that there was anything in Haitian art or in Haiti itself that was *not* primitive. How long could the new artists work knowing that no one seemed to be prepared to deal with the complexity of their creations? How long can you produce art when you believe that no one really wants to look at it?

Gabriel smiled, looking unperturbed, and asked if I had seen any of the local voodoo shows, the re-creations of the authentic services officially outlawed by the Baby Doc government, which were then offered around town to enlighten the tourists. I thought that maybe his English wasn't too good; maybe he hadn't understood anything of what I was saying. No, I said, I hadn't been to a voodoo re-creation. I don't like re-creations of anything.

Gabriel said that he understood, but that I must go. Because, he said, Haiti is an island of high magic. It was the only answer he would give me.

And so I went to the Péristyle de Mariani, a replica voodoo temple built out over the bay, to see the *houngan* draw the *vèvè* and summon *Agwé, loa* of the sea. I was not impressed. Oh, the ritual was fascinating, and the drums beat a compelling rhythm, and the red light blazed from the fire that billowed from around the center post, setting off the pure white dresses of the *hounsi*, the young girls who assisted the priest, chanting constantly and dancing the *yanvalu* with hems held high. And when the *loa* did supposedly come down and possess one of them, throwing her to the ground and then lifting her up and making her dance with frenzy and abandon, I could almost imagine what it must be like in the backcountry, beyond the view of the Haitian government and the French and American tourists, where such things happen for real. But only "almost." For as her sister priestesses led the girl away, I couldn't forget that she was going off to a dressing room somewhere to change into blue jeans and smoke a cigarette and think about the young man she would be meeting in the bar after the show.

I got up from my table and made my way to the bar and ordered another rum punch. I leaned back against the railing and looked out over the bay. The air was warm and whispered of the heat of midday. The breeze took the smoke from the fire out over the sea and somehow brought it back diluted with a pleasant aroma, seasoned with salt. I watched the *houngan* busy with his gyrations. And I thought, what a pity he can do this when it's not for real. Then I saw her, the *hounsi* who had (supposedly) been possessed. She was out there in the moonlit bay, her pure white dress billowing on the swell. She was well beyond the shallows, beyond the surf, in deep water. But she wasn't swimming; she was moving on the water with the slow grace of a fish or a mermaid—or a *loa* of the sea. And there was no one there to see her except me.

As it turned out, no one ever did see her. My article, after all, was supposed to be a 3,000-word travel piece keyed to Haitian art. It came to 3,500 words, and the scene at the Péristyle was deemed "peripheral." So that's what got cut. The fact is, I let it happen. I let the editors cut it because I needed this one; I was a nobody in the world of publishing, and I was just starting to get a reputation. I also needed the money, of course. Besides, it was only a travel magazine. Why cast pearls before swine?

At least that's what I told myself. And I told myself it was all right. But it wasn't all right. Because when I got my copy of the magazine I couldn't read the article. Not because the writing was bad, but because it wasn't what I had seen. There was fire in Haiti and I had left it there.

The effect of that girl, the sight of her, would come up later in my book *The Chaneysville Incident*. I had a scene where I wanted a Biblical allusion, and I was poking around in the Apocrypha in search of a nifty quote. In the Book of Esdras I came across this: "I shall light a candle of understanding in thy heart." And it impressed me. Not head, heart. Not cool intellect, but a flame of understanding. And I recognized that there was a theme hidden in my book as it then existed: the conflict between objective knowledge, which is the product of analysis and logic and data, and belief, which has no data, no analysis and no logic. The synthesis was understanding— something that combines knowledge and faith. I had a character in that book, a cold-eyed fellow named John Washington. I didn't think of it then, but he was just the kind of guy who could float up above everything and watch fire floating around. And what had to happen to him in that book was that he go down.

During the writing of *The Chaneysville Incident* my father died. I was one of the speakers who eulogized him, and in doing that I found out something else—that I could preach. I stood in the pulpit, looked at the congregation of people he had ministered to for twenty years, and realized that I couldn't say what I wanted to say, what *I* believed. I had to say what *he* believed. I called his death and burial "the Easter of my father." When I was finished, the bishop offered me a church. He was kidding, of course; he knew me. He said, "You sounded just like your father." And I said, "It *was* him."

The year after that I spent trying to become a freelance

writer. I failed miserably. Everything I wrote got rejected for very good reasons. I ended up going back to a job I swore I would never touch again. I also went back over the year of failure, trying to figure out what I had been able to do before that I wasn't doing now. I realized that what it was was to go inside. I realized that when I wrote *The Chaneysville Incident* I said a lot of things I didn't want to say, and I wanted to say a lot of things that I didn't really say. I decided to do it again.

The only way I could think to do it was to think of my father and his sermons. There's one in particular that I want to tell you about now. The year was 1965. By that time our summer travels had taken my father and me beyond Virginia into North and South Carolina, and in one place they asked my father to preach. I wasn't overly excited by the prospect, since I'd heard him preach maybe a thousand times and I'd always found his sermons to be rather dry, tending, as he tended, to focus on the head rather than the heart. The text was Isaiah 30:21: "And my ear shall be a word, ye shall hear a word behind thee, saying, This is the way. Walk ye in it."

As my father read it I realized that I had heard this sermon at least four times, liking it less each time. I expected the usual textual analysis and explication by definition that marked his style. But on this night he abandoned that. Something got hold of him, and he followed the reading of the text by telling a story. He said that as a boy in high school he was sitting in a classroom one day when a man came asking for volunteers to go and fight a forest fire that was raging on a nearby mountain. My father and some other young men agreed to go and were taken up the mountain by wagon. Then they went on foot a mile or two farther to a point where they were told to dig a firebreak. The fire seemed a long way away, and my father and his friends became absorbed in the task. When they finally looked up they found that the fire was all around them. They were surrounded by flames.

My father described his panic—how he had first cried hysterically and had then begun to curse, using words he hadn't realized he knew, and had finally collapsed in desperate prayer. It all seemed useless. But then, when the smoke was at its thickest, when he could no longer see his companions or even hear their wailing in the roar of the flames, there came a voice calling to them to follow. They followed that voice and escaped through what must have been the last gap in the fire. Afterward they asked who had risked himself to save them. But nobody could tell them who it was.

From that story my father moved to the obvious but eloquent equation, exchanging the unknown savior for a known one who calls the same message and who leads all who follow Him clear of the flames. Then, abruptly, and much sooner than anyone expected, he stopped. And he brought down the house.

That sermon shocked me. Because I knew my father. I knew he had hidden that story for forty years—had kept it out of previous versions of the sermon because he was a man who hated to admit weakness or indecision. I knew how expensive that sermon was for him. I knew that to relive that time on the mountainside had cost him greatly, and to admit his own helplessness had cost him even more.

But I also saw that it was the paying of that price that had made the sermon possible. In confessing his own weakness my father had found access to a hidden source of power inside, or perhaps outside, himself. In any case it was a source of power that was magical and mystical.

Until that night I had only understood that the writer's goal was to reveal truths in words manipulated so effectively as to cause movement in the minds and hearts of those who read them. What I hadn't understood was that it would cost anything. I thought I could do those things while remaining secure and safe in myself. I had even thought that writing fiction was a way to conceal my true feelings and weaknesses.

But that night I realized that no matter how good I became at manipulating symbols I could never hope to move anyone without allowing myself to be moved—that I would only arrive at slight truths if I wasn't willing to reveal truths about myself.

I didn't enjoy the realization, for I was no fonder of self-revelation than my father was. And although I knew I would love to do with written words what my father had done in speech, I wasn't sure I could pay the price. I wasn't sure I wanted to.

Eventually I would write about my father and his church, in an article that was published in the *New York Times*. I wasn't exactly afraid to write that piece. But even as I began it I was aware that I would be touching on the marrow of my bones, that I would be playing with fire. And even now I can't say too much about the process, except this: it's still going on. Not writing the piece—that was done two years ago—but writing, or rewriting, myself.

For that's where my understanding of all this has brought me. I understand why that science fiction novel didn't end when the fire came down. Because the ending could only come when that young man learned not to stand aloof, not just to watch the fire wash over him, but to feel it. I also suppose that's how Faulkner may have felt, how he captured the fire to reach across the barriers of generation and origin and race and kindle a light of understanding in my heart. What I had to do to be a writer was to be in two places at once—to both bring the fire and to allow it to wash over me, to change me and touch me and make me different.

It may sound silly, but I believe that to become a better writer I have to try to become a better person, just as I believe that the best preacher is not the saint but the person who allows himself or herself to be touched by the word, even as he or she transmits or interprets it. Of course a writer isn't really a preacher, and a novel isn't divine word. Every reading is not religious conversion. Every preacher is not a saint, God knows. Every sermon is not a masterpiece, and every sermon doesn't bring them screaming up to the altar. But the truth, I hope, is that we come to both a book and a service of worship with the same hopes—that we'll learn something, yes, but, more important, that we'll be touched by something, that we will feel a connection with some source of power and energy and understanding.

In *The Varieties of Religious Experience* William James defined several characteristics that he said were common to all religious belief. One is important here: that spiritual energy flows in and produces effects, psychological or material, within the phenomenal world. Those effects don't always have to be as powerful as the fire out of heaven that the science fiction author wrote about. Indeed, Mohammed, writing for Allah, as translated by Ahmed Ali, put it this way: "God is the light of the heavens and the earth. The semblance of his light is that of a niche which is in a lamp, the flame within a glass, the glass a glittering star."

As a writer, what I hope to do is to fill that little niche. But if you agree with James, then writing is my religion.

For I do believe that somehow, no matter what the writing task, no matter how interesting or straightforward the technique, no matter how mercenary the reasons for writing it, if I search my soul and my heart I will find a way to capture some kind of energy, to somehow bring down a little fire to change my readers and change myself.

A Messenger of Wonder

Because I often use religious words in my writing—words like grace and benediction and prayer—readers sometimes ask me about my own religious beliefs and are surprised to learn that I'm one of the most religious people I know. It's just that I don't happen to believe in a governing God. I don't need to believe in God to have a devastating amount of respect, even awe, for the universe and the creatures that inhabit it and for the subtlety of matter. When I say "subtlety" I think of how often people refer to *mere* matter. But the fact that matter can result in the loopy weather system of a child's fingerprints—that's not mere; that's extraordinary.

There are different terms I suppose you could apply to my brand of spirituality. You might call it eco-spirituality. I think of myself as an earth ecstatic. It's my own private church, and the creed is simple. I believe in the sanctity of all life and in the perfectibility of people. For me it suggests that human beings, though breathtakingly complex and resplendent, can improve their behavior toward one another and the planet, and that all of existence is sacred. I don't require a deity for that stance. Even without an organized religion or a church I often find myself in a position of praise or prayer.

I also find myself constantly going on pilgrimages and quests. One of my essays describes my quest for the last of the short-tailed albatrosses. I knew that it was going to mean traveling to the tiny island of Torishima, 600 kilometers south of Tokyo—working my way down the Japanese island chain to get there and leaving from one of those last handholds that human beings have always embarked from, beyond which everything is unknown. (It used to be St. Louis in the old days in America.) You rent a fishing boat and head out for an island that's only a mile and a half wide. You have to go in monsoon season, because that's the nesting season of the birds, and you may have to swim through water that's full of sharks to reach the shore. Then you climb a rock face ten stories high to get to an abandoned garrison, where you leave your things, and then you hike across the active volcano and let yourself down 400 feet by rope into a fortress of stone. That's when you see the birds.

Nobody told me there was going to be this 400-foot rope descent without any harness. The two men I traveled with were experienced rock climbers. I don't have upper-body strength, and I slipped—luckily I hung onto the rope—and swung back and hit the cliff and broke three ribs. At that point my life became very, very difficult. I managed to get down, but I couldn't move the upper half of my body. So my two companions dug a pit in the volcanic sand, and that's where I watched the birds from. I just sat there like a monk, most of that day and the next day, beholding them.

There is a form of beholding that is a kind of prayer; I felt that, very powerfully. And although my companions didn't go through as much hell as I did, they went through a lot; it's not easy to have to deal with someone who is as broken up as I was and try to get her back to civilization. But I think they believed me when I told them it was worth the pain to see those beautiful birds: to see a rare life-form that may vanish in my lifetime. As I said to them, who would drink from the cup when you can drink from the source? I also wanted to celebrate the birds; I didn't want them to die without someone bearing witness to how extraordinary they are. The liturgy in my church of earth ecstasy includes more than a sense of gratitude; I also believe in celebration as a way to proselytize. If I can make people fall in love with an endangered animal they'll fight to save it.

The albatross piece was one of many quests for severely endangered animals that eventually went into my book, *The Rarest of the Rare: Vanishing Animals, Timeless Worlds.* Some of the other quests were a trip to the Amazon; an expedition to Northern Brazil with golden lion tamarins that we intended to turn loose in the wild; and a trip to a tiny endangered ecosystem in the Florida scrublands. On one remote island in the Hawaiian archipelago I tagged and doctored monk seals. That book turned out to be a sequel to my earlier book, *The Moon by Whale Light and Other Adventures Among Crocodilians, Whales, Penguins and Bats,* which took me to remote sites as far away as Antarctica.

In both books I talk in my introduction about what it's like to be a nature writer, and how peculiar and enticing it is to live on seasonal time, and about some of the other illusions and paradoxes you have to adopt when you do this kind of work. For example, you have to be willing to enter an alternate reality which has its own social customs and values, and that can mean leaving all the guideposts and routines you once relied on far behind you.

I don't go on such extreme scientific trips anymore; I've broken too many bones and have been close to death too often. But in my more recent books I've been doing something similar, which is to work with my favorite animal, the human. In 1995 I had a broken foot that wouldn't heal for two years, so I couldn't go out on an expedition. Instead I undertook a National Geographic gray squirrel project. I captured all the squirrels in my backyard, ear-tagged them, gave them colored necklaces and studied their ways and relationships. At the same time I began doing volunteer work as a telephone counselor at a suicide-prevention crisis center.

The book that eventually resulted from that double experience, *A Slender Thread*, is my favorite kind of inquiry. It looks at nature and human nature, but especially at the crossroads where they meet and have something to say about each other. By day I would work with the squirrels and by night I would work with the people calling in on the telephone hotline. Both groups had the same motives and the same fears; they were all looking for attachments, and they were all concerned about loss of resources, or status: things like that. The animals got depressed just as the people did. It helped me see the human saga against the backdrop of the rest of the animal world that we belong to, which I've come to know and love. Almost everything dangerous or poignant that can happen to people prompted a telephone call to the crisis center—from depression, suicide and murder to all the trials, uncertainties and conflicts of love. But the work wasn't at all depressing; it was uplifting.

Altogether I spent five years at the crisis center, part time, and it was the most rewarding work I've ever done. What was thrilling was that the work was anonymous. There was no applause. You weren't proving yourself to anyone. You were making contact with people you would never meet, whose faces you would never see, at some of the most raw and perilous moments of their lives.

I also learned about altruism and what an important part it plays in our emotions. You don't read much about that in the newspapers; we're taught by society that our species is mainly warlike. But now I know there are these anonymous armies of the day and night under the surface of every American city, performing acts of heroism and mercy for their neighbors whom they will never meet. In many ways it's analogous to the monastic or the cloistered life. Whenever I was doing that counseling I was aware that it was like being in a confessional: the telephone, with its perforations, into which people were pouring out their heart in the most intimate way. You're all alone in that room, and the stories are pushed against your ear; it just feeds into your soul. I felt that it was a sacramental transaction.

What made it bizarre was that I was leading a double existence. The telephone counseling was the most urgent, emotionally exhausting and meaningful thing going on in my life, but I couldn't talk about it publicly, and I couldn't write about it. At the same time, however, I was writing my other books. Finally there came a point, in 1997, when I realized that I could probably help more people if I did go public with the suicide-prevention work, and I wrote *A Slender Thread*. Fortunately, that hunch turned out to be true. I've heard from many readers about their own struggles and how my book gave them comfort and hope.

But writing the book also helped *me*. It made it easier for me to write about my own life far more candidly. In my earlier writings I'm not the hero; everybody else is the hero. I don't like being the hero. First of all, I don't feel like a hero. Also, trying to be larger than life isn't what excites me. What excites me is seeing the world through someone else's sensibility, or through the sensibility of an animal. But because of the confidentiality rules at the suicide-prevention center I couldn't tell the story of the hotline callers from their point of view, or from the other counselors' point of view. That meant that, in a fictional sense, I was the main character. So I ended up revealing and exploring more areas of my past than I ever had before. It was a transitional book; I became more exposed and began taking more and more chances.

That trend continues in my next book, *Deep Play*. It's about only one facet of my personality, but a very powerful one. I believe that play underlies what most human beings do with their lives. My book is about the whole world of play, but especially ecstatic play—the transcendent form of play that makes thrill-seeking understandable, makes creativity possible, and makes religion inevitable. I explore our passion to transcend ourselves and to enter into a religious state, whatever area of play we're driven to pursue. For some people it could be stamp collecting, or driving racing cars.

In any case, the enterprise is sacred. All playgrounds are sacred places, and all sacred places are playgrounds. My book talks about the human need for pilgrimage and the surprising fact that so many places all over the world have been designated as sacred; something like 80 percent of travel is a pilgrimage to famous churches and religious sites and other holy places. Why do we need the holy in our lives? I'm interested in how that question works itself out through play, especially how those of us who have turned away from organized religions have sought to fill that need somewhere else.

For some people that place is sports, which they pursue with religious fervor. If we're very lucky, we're also able to make play our work. Not all artists rise to that estate, but many do, and I'm sure that's part of the appeal of being an artist. My book also looks at thrill-seeking, an extreme form of play. All games involve risk and tension; they're held in a special place set off from the rest of the world, where certain rules apply and there's a morality that is specific to the game. The philosopher Jeremy Bentham dismissed as "deep play" any activities in which you stand to lose more than you stand to gain, so why would anyone perform them? But the more I thought about that, the more I realized that not only have I spent my life involved in those activities; most people do. They live for those moments, those quests.

People on quests are a big element in my book. One of them, for instance, is Gauguin, whose art was a lifelong quest that took the form of an actual pilgrimage, to French Polynesia. I describe one trip that I made to the Bahamas with a group of people to study spotted dolphins. Every day the dolphins would come in to play with us. They'd come up and get you to follow them, and they'd go tighter, tighter, tighter in a circle, and then they'd peel off and watch you. Or I would toss my hair ribbon to one of them, and the dolphin would flip it back to me. It was clearly a game, and they played these games with us all the time. I don't know what was going on in the minds of the dolphins, but the intention of the humans was to have a bond with a wild animal in its own element. There was something profoundly spiritual about it. Afterward, when the people talked about those encounters, it was with a rapture that threw the whole world into focus. They had been given a clarity of the kind that many religious people have reported when they go up into the mountains, or on their walkabouts.

For me, writing about play or transcendence or the dark night of the soul just puts into place one more piece of the puzzle. I may seem to have written many books, but it's always the same book, the same puzzle. I think of it as a water table. You have all this underground water, and maybe there'll be a well over here that animals are drinking from, and a well over there that people are drinking from, and a well over here that feeds a city system, but ultimately it's the same water, the same source. In retrospect, I see that I've been trying to put together a mosaic of life on earth, breaking up the experience of being alive into manageable fragments and addressing them one by one: what it was like to have once been alive on the planet, what it felt like, what it tasted like, what it smelled like, what it thrilled like. Joshua Heschel, a very interesting rabbi and mystic, said he didn't pray for faith; he prayed for wonder. That is also my prayer. Wonder is the heaviest element on the periodic table; a tiny fleck of it stops time. My periodic table of the heart also has many other elements, still unidentified by science. One of them is "unattainium." That's the one that continues to drive us forward whether or not we expect to succeed.

I suppose it's in my poetry that I come closest to expressing my need for a spiritual life as well as a physical life.

I think of these lines, for instance, from my poem "School Prayer":

I swear I will not dishonor
my soul with hatred,
but offer myself humbly
as a guardian of nature,
as a healer of misery,
as a messenger of wonder,
as an architect of peace. . . .

I will honor all life
—wherever and in whatever form
it may dwell—on Earth my home,
and in the mansions of the stars.

I believe in the separation of church and state; I don't want children forced to worship someone else's God. But then they often end up with no spirituality at all. So I was trying in that poem to devise a school prayer that didn't include any organized religion or supernatural deity but that still entailed commitment and values. It bothers me that modern religion is not very religious. Most religions are based on the teachings of people who had visions and were profoundly moved by what happened to them. But their teachings have since passed into the hands of people who in many cases haven't experienced such inspiration themselves; much of the original intensity and awe and urgency have been lost. If the founders of the various religions were to walk into churches today expressing those ideas they would be cast out as crazy people. Yet what we all long for is a deep sense of connectedness—of ourselves as small beings in a huge and powerful universe, surrounded by forces we know very little about.

I write more prose than anything else, but the source of my creativity continues to be as a poet. Sometimes I insinuate what I think of as unrequited poems into my prose and hope nobody will notice. And sometimes I'm writing paragraphs and I don't know if they're prose or poetry. That blurred edge seems to be true for many poets who also write prose. Dylan Thomas, for instance. Or Rilke. When you read Rilke's prose you know you're in the presence of a poet's obsessions and sensibility. I think I have a poet's obsession, too. I often feel a greater sense of reward from writing a poem and being able to condense onto one page something I've been trying to get at than from writing pages of prose about it.

Because I write so much about the natural sciences, people often ask me whether I have a unifying view of science and nature and space and the environment. My answer is that I take the universe literally. As one verse. I find all of it fascinating, and I find it fascinating in detail. So I've never been able to draw a line between so-called science on one side and so-called nature on the other—human doings or scientific doings. It's all part of the same continuum. It's been just as fulfilling for me to write about quarks as to write about cornflowers. I'm aware that many people regard science as the spoilsport of feeling. But what fascinates me about science are its revelations, not the enterprise itself.

My next-door neighbor is a high-energy physicist, one of the very few women high-energy physicists in the world. She and I good-naturedly disagree about something. She believes there are absolute truths that are knowable by science. Her professional life is committed to the pursuit of those truths, and she believes that they would be authentic anywhere in the universe—that they are universal truths. I, on the other hand, believe that science is simply a different language, a different way of knowing—one at which human beings excel. Trapped inside the beautiful prison of our sensibilities, we can only know what we know within those limits. Therefore what she calls truth I think is only truth for us. Beings elsewhere in the universe might experience reality differently. I see it as very subjective. So I can't keep science out of my work, because it's part of the universe, but I'm not making a conscious choice to pursue it, and I believe in it as I believe in art. I want the truths that both the sciences and the arts can teach me.

The tradition that I write out of, I think, is largely an American tradition: writers like Walt Whitman and Loren Eiseley. I also feel close to writer-scientists like Lewis Thomas. In the British tradition it would be people like John Donne and the other Metaphysicals. Their minds were like upside-down umbrellas; everything poured in. My muse is a miscellaneous muse. I'm a nomadic writer; my curiosity is always picking up its tent and traveling and pitching itself someplace else. But the journey continues to be the same, whichever direction it's going in and whatever challenges the different landscapes offer.

JAROSLAV PELIKAN

Writing as a Means of Grace

In the beginning was the word. *En archē ēn bo logos.* Anybody who has taken a semester of Greek has learned that. Those are the opening words of the Gospel of John, and you will recall—that's what a professor says when he's not sure people will recall—that Goethe's Faust struggled with the meaning of those words at the very beginning of the play: "*Im Anfang war das Wort . . . der Sinn . . . die Kraft . . . die Tat.*" "In the beginning was the word, the meaning, the power, the deed."

In the beginning was the word. This is of course one of the most shattering metaphysical statements in the New Testament, and more than any other statement it provides the basis for the Christian doctrine of the Trinity. But it's not only a metaphysical statement. With its roots simultaneously in the Hebrew and the Greek tradition—in the Hebrew tradition, where the very first act of God in the first chapter of the first book of the Bible is to speak, and in the Greek tradition, where the word for "word" and the word for "reason" are the same—this declaration affirms that the act of communication is at the very center not only of human existence and its origins but of the mystery of the Divine Being itself. And so the transmission of the word, the moving of the word from within to without, from the word that dwells within to the word that emerges, *logos endiatbetos* to *logos propborikos*—the mystery of that process is the mystery of divine communication and of divine self-communication, and therefore of the Divine Self.

Human beings, being created, according to that first chapter of the first book of the Bible, in the divine image, in the image of a God who has no face, participate through the divine image in the mystery of the Divine Being by reflecting those capacities of the Divine Being that lie at the center of self-revelation. And those capacities are two, but finally they are one: the capacity to love and the capacity to communicate. For in the beginning was the word.

I want to talk to you today about three sensitive, thoughtful, troubled writers in whose own lives the mystery of the word, of its communication through speech and especially through writing, played a decisive role.

Within Western culture, more perhaps than any other non-Biblical book *The Confessions of St. Augustine* participates in that mystery. One has only to try to find antecedents for Augustine's confessions to realize that this is—to use an overworked word—a unique book. Its nearest analogy for centuries before it is *The Meditations of Marcus Aurelius*, and if you read the two books side by side, as I did with a group of undergraduates a few years ago, you realize that they are altogether different in their outlook, method and style.

For *The Confessions of St. Augustine* is one single uninterrupted sentence. It could be punctuated with semicolons all the way to the end. This single sentence, moreover, is written in the second person singular. For *The Confessions*, as the very title suggests, is a prayer, addressed to God—addressed to Augustine's God, a God to whom it was not possible to lie. For that God already knew what Augustine was trying to dredge up out of his memory. But it was also a God to whom it was not necessary to lie. For the God who knew the deepest and darkest recesses of Augustine's soul was also a God of grace and forgiveness. And it is in the permissive atmosphere of grace, in the context of forgiveness, that Augustine lays bare his soul—for God and for anybody else who might look over his shoulder at the book.

So in its literary form *The Confessions* stands as a piece of introspection—in some sense or other an autobiography, or, if you like, a spiritual autobiography. But perhaps the best term for it is the term that was chosen as the title for this series of talks. It is a spiritual quest—a quest for meaning, for coherence, for integrity. It describes a quest as Augustine moved from one preoccupation to another, from preoccupation with self to a dozen years as a member of the murky Manichean sect, to various kinds of neo-Platonism, to orthodox Christianity, always questing.

Behind that quest he believed was a yet deeper quest—a quest *by* the Divine, by the Almighty; a quest for Augustine and for every other soul. *God in Search of Man* is the title of a book by my late friend Rabbi Abraham Heschel, and that's also the theme of Augustine's book. For Augustine, like a later English poet, Francis

Thompson, fled the hound of heaven but was pursued down the corridors of his own life.

With that as his intent, Augustine undertakes in *The Confessions* a very special methodology. In the first Epistle to the Corinthians, in the thirteenth chapter, Paul says, "Now we see through a glass darkly," and many people think that means a window. Of course it doesn't; it means a mirror: "Now we see in a mirror, darkly" (*per speculum in aenigmate*). If you've ever seen mirrors from the Hellenistic and Roman period you know that people did indeed see in them very darkly, and one wonders how Cleopatra ended up as beautiful as she did with that kind of mirror.

Augustine takes that statement—we see *"per speculum,"* in a mirror—and makes it the methodological key to his enterprise; namely, that if you want to look at the face of God, in whose presence all living things will shrivel and die, you must do what you do if you want to watch an eclipse of the sun. You must find some place where the light is reflected but where it is also tamped down.

And he finds that place not only in nature, and not only in human history—after all, he did write *The City of God*—but also, finally, within his own soul. And in this book he undertakes to study his own soul and to read off from his soul the data that will tell him what God is and what God does. And so in that sense the book is an account of Augustine's relations with God—of God's patience with him, of how God pushed him in one direction or another, of how he resisted ("Oh Lord, make me chaste, but not yet"), of how he moved from one place to another (T. S. Eliot paraphrased him, "To Carthage came I burning, burning"), and finally how that restlessness was a means of grace. "Thou hast made us for Thyself," he writes, "and our heart is restless until it finds its rest in Thee." And it did.

Augustine writes from the perspective of someone who has found the goal and who now proceeds to describe the quest, attempting to relive the events of that quest and therefore probing as no one ever did before him and as, after him, no one did again until Sigmund Freud probed, as Augustine put it, "the mystery of memory by which the past becomes present to me, by which the sins of the past, their pleasure and gratification, can be present to me now, and if not in my conscious mind then in my dreams, in which I all but relive them." Augustine proceeds to discern a direction and a pattern in all of that, for he believes that he is able to find the hand of God guiding and at the same time waiting. For this was a God who created humanity, but who created humanity free enough even to defy the divine will.

In the Middle Ages they used to ask—they had nothing much else to do, so they asked such questions—"Can God create a stone so heavy that God himself cannot lift it?" And if you say No, he cannot, then of course God is not almighty because he can't create such a stone. And if you say Yes, he can, then of course God is not almighty because he can't lift such a stone. Well, the answer to that question in Augustine, as indeed in the Hebrew Bible, is quite simple. Yes, there is such a stone: it is the human will, created by God, but created in such a way that God cannot lift it. For, as Augustine says, God does not rape; God woos, and therefore God will take his chances on winning or losing and will finally prefer to let someone be lost rather than to interfere with the sacredness of the human person.

So this process of "reading off" is what impels the writing of *The Confessions*. They are a rehearsal, a reenactment, but as seen *"per speculum."* So convinced was Augustine of the validity of this method that already in *The Confessions*, and then especially in the most profound of his speculative works, the treatise on the Trinity, he was prepared to find in the human soul an analogy for the Trinity itself: to see in the relation between intellect, will and love, and in similar kinds of connections, the working out of the image of the Trinity—the "footsteps" of the Trinity, as he calls them, *Vestigia Trinitatis*—in the human soul.

Writing *The Confessions*, then, was—and this isn't intended to be a pun—a confession. In Augustine and in the Hebrew Bible the word "confession" has a two-fold meaning. On the one hand it's a confession of sin, a laying bare of one's self to one's confessor in order to be shriven, as, for example, in the 51st Psalm of David. And it's also a confession of faith, of faith in the God who created, who judges and who forgives. And all of that is put together into a book, one of the few books from antiquity that have never been out of style. Every century since Augustine's death in 430 has read his *Confessions* with delight. That's not true of Plato's *Republic*, of Aristotle's *Metaphysics*, of Cicero's *Orations*, or even of Caesar's *Commentaries on the Gallic War*. (Every generation did read Caesar's *Gallic War*, but under some constraint.)

But Augustine's *Confessions* have been read over and over again by the crazy mixed-up kids of every generation, regardless of their age. Because in this act of writing, the narrative of grace becomes itself a means of grace, and by following the steps through which Augustine moved, or through which God led him, we ourselves see where we are in the schema of divine grace and forgiveness, and we find there both the mystery of Augustine's personality, the mystery of our own personality, and, if you wish, the mystery of the Divine Being. *The Confessions* are a conversion narrative. They tell a story with a beginning and a middle and an end—or at least an end as of the writing of the book, with more still to come.

One of the most important conversion narratives of modern times also has a Latin title, though the treatise itself is in English. It's the *Apologia pro Vita Sua (Defense of His Own Life)* by John Henry Newman. Newman was an Oxford don, a promising young scholar in Greek who had edited various Greek writings and had also shown himself to be a master of English prose. In 1844-45 Newman wrote his *Essay on the Development of Christian Doctrine*, a treatise that has been extremely important to me in my own scholarship. In it he sought to identify some of the patterns by which Christian doctrine had developed from one century to another. That research led him to the conclusion that what had kept Christian doctrine from developing wrongly was the guiding hand of the See of Rome, and therefore in 1845 John Henry Newman, on the basis of his own scholarship, became a Roman Catholic and set the pattern for various English-speaking writers, notably G. K. Chesterton, to move in the same direction ever since.

Newman described his conversion at length in a *roman à clef* called *Loss and Gain*, published (anonymously) in 1848. In that novel a sensitive young man with an Oxford background and literary esthetic tastes finally comes to the conclusion that the only place where he can find peace for his soul is within the bosom of Mother Church, and as a result he proceeds to realign his relations with his family and his friends. Some of them try to understand, and do; some of them try to understand, and don't; some of them don't even want to understand.

The young man's relationship to each of them becomes the stuff of that novel. It's also, though in a much more substantial and scholarly way, the stuff of the later *Apologia pro Vita Sua*. For Newman became very much a *cause célèbre* in the 1850s and '60s when he was vigorously attacked from both right and left. Many of the attacks came from old-line Roman Catholics, who weren't at all sure that his conversion was genuine, who were quite sure that what he had been converted to was not the Catholicism they had grown up with. For the Catholicism of John Henry Newman comes much closer to the spirit of the Second Vatican Council than the First. Indeed, it was said in Rome in the 1960s that at last Cardinal Newman has his council. For at Vatican II, unlike Vatican I, what prevailed was the organic sense of the total growth of the Christian community, rather than the juridical sense of a church that legislated doctrine for its believers. In Newman's time it was that juridical sense which dominated the first Vatican Council of 1869 and 1870. That was the party line. Therefore many Roman Catholics weren't convinced by Newman's conversion.

On the other hand, his Anglican friends—his liberal and secular friends—couldn't understand why anybody who obviously had as many brains as John Henry Newman did could let himself in for anything as obscurantist as becoming a Roman Catholic. The attacks on him therefore came from all directions—for instance, from Charles Kingsley, author of *Westward Ho!*, who, in a series of articles, raised questions about the fundamental moral integrity of Newman and of his belief about truth. Kingsley accused Newman of having said that in the interests of achieving a religious goal it was permissible to fudge on the truth. Augustine had once said, "Remember that God never needs our lies." Think about that, if you've been parents, and think about what such a principle would amount to in the course of the twenty years you spend answering children's questions. It's a shattering imperative.

In response to all those attacks, Newman was obliged not only to clarify what he meant by his own view of truth and falsehood, but to tell the story of his conversion. He subtitled his *Apologia* "A History of My Religious Opinions." In many ways it is patterned after Augustine's *Confessions*. It's written in the kind of English that Augustine would have written if he had gone to Oxford. But, more profoundly, it is in the tradition of the *Confessions* as a subjective document, describing what Newman believes to be an objective reality. Therefore it adopts Augustine's method of "reading off" the story of his childhood and youth, and looks by hindsight for indications, all along the road, of the process that had brought him to 1845 and beyond.

The *Apologia* is therefore a remarkable exercise for the writer, but also for the reader. For inevitably in such a process, as was already true of Augustine, there's a selectivity in the events that are "important"—the events that in one way or another anticipate or sometimes by contrast highlight the way the story came out, now that we know how it did come out.

There's a certain age at which people write such books. They have become to some extent public figures; their persona is largely determined and fixed, and now as writers they begin to sift the story for those objective-subjective data that will make sense out of the higgledy-piggledy events of a life. One man who did that earlier in the nineteenth century when he had become a persona, if not an icon, was Johann Wolfgang von Goethe. He subtitled his autobiography *Dichtung und Warbeit* (Fiction and Truth). For he knew and candidly admitted that the very process of selecting makes such a work a work of fiction.

The *Apologia* of Newman, therefore, is an attempt, made at what might be called the other end of the Christian era, to do what Augustine had done at the beginning of the Christian era of European history. For if that era begins in the fourth century with the conversion of Constantine (and that, after all, was only a few years before Augustine's birth), and if it ends somewhere at the beginning of the nineteenth century with Napoleon or Goethe or Darwin, Newman's *Apologia* comes at that ending point and attempts to reenact in his own life the forces by which his generation had been alienated from the Christian tradition and the processes by which the tradition could be recovered.

So that, too, is a spiritual quest—a quest for meaning, integrity, memory; a quest to understand the mystery of his conversion and to communicate it in a way that others, like his friends in *Loss and Gain*, will, if not understand, at least respect or forgive.

Almost exactly a century after Augustine died—in 430, as you will recall—Boethius, the last of the Romans, a consul of the Roman Republic, was imprisoned for treason to the emperor. He was a scholar, one of the last major figures in the West who moved with equal ease in both Latin and Greek. Knowing Greek was a rare accomplishment in early Western scholarship. Dante, for example, didn't know *The Iliad* and *The Odyssey*, and throughout the Middle Ages the only dialogue of Plato that was known was the *Timaeus* because it was available in Latin. For a thousand years most scholars in the West didn't know any Greek.

What they did know of the Greek tradition they knew through a couple of figures, primarily Boethius. For Boethius as a young man dreamed big dreams. He would, he hoped, translate all of Aristotle from Greek into Latin, translate all of Plato from Greek into Latin, and then write a system that would harmonize the differences between the two, and do all this in the spirit of the Christian gospel.

He didn't quite make it. What he did translate were the logical writings of Aristotle, what we now call the *Organon*, and that was why through the Middle Ages Aristotle was remembered in the West as a logician. It was only when the Arabs translated Aristotle from Greek into Arabic and some Christians then rendered that Arabic into Latin, thereby reintroducing the metaphysical writings of Aristotle in the twelfth and thirteenth centuries, that the real Aristotle came through. Eventually he was translated from Greek directly into Latin, in a form that made it possible for Saint Thomas Aquinas to write the *Summa Theologica*. But until then Boethius's translation of the Greek logical writings of Aristotle into Latin was all that was known of his work.

A scholar and public figure, Boethius, for a variety of reasons—primarily palace intrigue—got into trouble, was arrested, imprisoned and threatened with execution. And it was while he was in prison that he wrote his best-known book, the only one that anybody except specialists reads today—*The Consolation of Philosophy*. The plot of the book is that while languishing in prison in despair he is visited by Lady Philosophy, who, alternating prose and poetry, explains to him the meaning of faith, providence and free will and thus gives him reassurance even as he faces the prospect of death. One of my students in a seminar we had on Boethius a few years ago kept referring to this vision of the lady, Boethius's imaginary friend, as "sort of like Harvey." So I can't read Boethius now without thinking of that rabbit in Mary Chase's play.

This vision gives Boethius an opportunity to explore within himself the resources of insight, faith and hope that will prepare him for he knows not what. *The Consolation of Philosophy* had an unbelievable influence on European thought and literature. Dante knew it by heart. I've just finished teaching a seminar on Dante's *Paradiso*, along with a colleague who is chairman of the Italian department at Yale, and it was my job to provide the footnotes, since Dante doesn't provide footnotes, and to look for echoes of Dante's reading, including, above all, *The Consolation* of Boethius. That influence is everywhere. It's also everywhere in Thomas Aquinas.

The Consolation was translated into Anglo-Saxon by King Alfred and translated into English by Geoffrey Chaucer. Then it was translated into English again, by Queen Elizabeth—the First, that is. As far as I know, it has never been out of print in five centuries, and it still bears careful reading. But there's no way to tell from the book that the author was a Christian. There's not a single reference to the person of Jesus, no allusion to the Cross, no clear quotation from either the New Testament or the Old. Not the Book of Job, which you might think would come to his mind, or the Psalms, which do after all deal with the question of why must the pious suffer, or Saint Paul sitting in prison writing his captivity letters. None of that. Instead the book proceeds completely on the basis of our common human experience and destiny and seeks to make sense of it. It's monotheistic, but in its monotheism it talks about *fatum* (fate) and *providentia* (providence) and seeks to show that *fatum* is subordinate to *providentia* and that therefore we must have hope and that we can do something about our condition, regardless of the restrictions that fate may place upon it.

That problem of the non-Christian character of *The Consolation* doesn't appear to have troubled anybody in the Middle Ages, or at least I haven't found any medieval scholars who wondered about it. In modern times, however, it has been a major historical and literary puzzle. For a long time German scholars—who tend to do that sort of thing—were sure that the author of *The Consolation* was different from the author of all the other theological treatises attributed to Boethius. Then at the beginning of the twentieth century a dissertation by an American professor, E. K. Rand, demonstrated on purely literary grounds that it was indeed the same person. Thus the problem of the authorship and the nature of this spiritual quest came dead center.

Today, if you read *The Consolation of Philosophy* knowing who and what the author was and remembering the title, you see that it's almost a pun. For in one sense the consolation is the consolation that Philosophy provides. "Harvey," this imaginary friend whose name is Philosophia, consoles and comforts; that's the consolation. And note that it's philosophy, not theology, that is the consolation. Boethius undoubtedly prayed while he was in prison; he says some things about that, and he may well have used the Psalms when he prayed. But here he's trying to answer the question of whether, even apart from divine revelation, simply by probing the nature of the human spirit in relation to the Divine Spirit, it's possible to find a philosophy that consoles. And he comes to the conclusion that it is possible—that the very structure of the world and the structure of the mind would require us to have a sense of direction and providence.

But the title is even more of a pun than that, for it is

not only capital *P* "Philosophy" and lower case *p* "philosophy." It is "Consolation." And when you finish the book you suddenly realize where the consolation came from. It came from writing the book. The very act of writing, the kind of dredging up of these questions and these tentative answers out of the past and out of the inner self—that very process, putting it down, trying to say it right, is the consolation. And so it is in the work of writing the work that the consolation comes, as it is in the quest that the finding comes. For a spiritual quest means precisely that: not starting in a vacuum at square one, but starting where we are with what we have and with what we have found, to quest for it again. In Augustine's beautiful term, it is *fides quaerens intellectum*— faith in search of understanding—so that, having found understanding, faith can search yet again. Over and over.

"Lead, kindly light, amid the encircling doom; lead thou me on" was Cardinal Newman's best-known prayer. For it is in the quest that we find; it is in the finding that we seek, not only because in the beginning was the word, but because the same word is also there at the end. *Devar Adonai leolam:* "The word of the Lord abideth forever."

PATRICIA HAMPL

Crying Out in Silence

Even to myself I'm an unlikely spiritual writer. When people describe me that way I still think they can't be talking about me.

I grew up in a very parochial, provincial place—St. Paul, Minnesota, the place F. Scott Fitzgerald couldn't wait to leave and successfully escaped from. The St. Paul I grew up in wasn't very different from the one he fled. Catholicism was something you could feel in the air— part of the ether we breathed. In that closed environment I don't think I met a "non-Catholic" (as we called them) until I went to the university. So I was like Fitzgerald in not being able to think of anything but getting out. It was my express desire to escape St. Paul, to escape Catholicism, to jettison everything those two very hovering places and institutions had given me.

And I succeeded. While I was attending a Catholic girl's convent school I applied to the University of Minnesota. That was a radical thing to do, because you were supposed to go to a Catholic school, and, best of all, a Catholic women's school. The directress called me down—a little bitty nun. She said, "Patricia, it has come to our attention that you have applied to the university. Do you realize that you will lose your faith over there?" And in my heart I thought, "Oh, yes!" This is what I wanted.

So I went to the university and set about becoming a writer. I didn't join the Newman Club—I had nothing to do with anything Catholic—and I succeeded in breaking my parents' hearts. Poetry became my religion. My attitude about literature was that it was a vocation: you dedicated your life to it and everything else was secondary. I went about being a '60s radical, and having a boyfriend who went to prison for avoiding the draft, and sitting in the street protesting various things, and getting involved in early feminism, and writing my poems and working on the student newspaper and other literary publications.

I now see that all of that was done with religious fervor. But I didn't darken a church or think of myself as a religious person. I made it clear to my parents that I was having no truck with Catholicism. My mother was saying the rosary for me, off in a corner, and my father didn't say anything at all. It went on that way for years. One day my mother said, "When are you going to come back to your religion?" And I spat out at her: "I'm more religious than you are." And I remember thinking, "Where on earth did that come from?" At that moment I realized that I still viewed life through a religious lens and that it hadn't been this great escape after all. I was still held within this whole environment while pretending to be away from it. I was still even living in St. Paul.

Finally I was pulled back into actual religious practice—into the inevitable human drama that people now call spirituality—by the Psalms. I was drawn to the Psalms because they had the ring of authenticity. I came to them as a poet looking at poetry, but also as someone with a broken heart looking for comfort. It wasn't just a literary enterprise; I went there instinctively.

What I found in the Psalms was what you only get, I think, from ancient voices being read in a contemporary setting: a shiver of recognition that the human experience is linked through the ages, and that it's linked mainly through language. These Psalms, which I had previously lumped with all the "religious" things I wanted nothing to do with, were in fact the crucible of the deepest human experience: love, betrayal, rancor, joy, radiance, misery, fury, pettiness. All the good stuff and all the bad stuff, in the deepest and mostly richly colored ways—it was in those Psalms. I couldn't keep away from them. I went around saying to my friends, "Have you read Psalm 88?" And they looked at me and thought, "What's happening to her?" And I'd say, "You haven't? What about 92?" I loved the Psalms because they didn't consist of the bromides that are usually associated with religion. I was comforted by the evidence of all those deep emotions having already been lived and suffered and yelled about by all those long gone but still vibrant people.

I also came to see that the Psalms represent one of the deepest continuing practices in Christian monastic tradition. Ordinarily, when we think of Catholicism we think, There's this thing called the Mass every Sunday, and that's the center of it all. But although it's the central drama, it's not the central cycle. All over the world in monastic settings, groups of people are going through a formal, patterned cycle of chanting and praying their way through those 150 poems, and doing it seasonally, doing it hourly. I was a goner when I put those two pieces together: the idea of time being controlled by poetry: It's funny it took me so long—I was about thirty-five—because I had been brought up by cloistered contemplative nuns who not only taught us, but who lived by that calendar. Making that connection was the start of my deep involvement. I found a monastery and began going there. I realized that I wanted to write a book about the contemplative life—the book that became *Virgin Time*.

The monastery that I found was called San Damiano and was in a suburb of Minneapolis, near a car dealership—a very unlikely place. I met a woman there who was very comic, or, I suppose, ironic. Sister Mary Madonna. She got a kick out of me, because I walked in there and told her: "I really don't want to have anything to do with Catholicism. But I think there's something here. I'm interested in the Psalms, and I want to write a book about monastic life. I'd like to come here and live for six months."

Well, imagine if I said to you, "I really like the way you and your family live; I'd like to move in." She looked at me as if I were crazy. "Why don't you just come on Sunday?" she said, and that began a long process of not looking at monastic life simply as a subject, but as something that had a relationship for me. I realized that my book was not going to be about monasticism, but about my struggle with Catholicism—the idea of growing up in the bubble of faith I grew up in, and then breaking out of the bubble.

From a literary point of view that repelled me, because it's easy to make fun of Catholicism. There have been so many good and not-so-good books about it—the "memories of a Catholic girlhood" genre. Suddenly it occurred to me that when people talk about religion they start by asking, "Do you believe in God?" And I thought: That question doesn't interest me in the least. But I do know that we have an instinct to pray—to praise, to plead, to cry out. There's also an instinct towards the kind of silence that's in the middle of prayer. When that thought came to me, the relationship between poetry and prayer became so close that I couldn't see the space in between. That's when I knew what my book would *really* be about: Why do people pray at the end of the twentieth century? What is contemporary prayer?

I also understood that the book must have a protagonist. Me. A memoir requires that you as the writer become not a hero or a heroine, because that would make it boring, the way narcissism is always boring. But you become the action figure, the struggling figure. I would have to talk about my own relationship to prayer. It would be an almost journalistic approach: What is prayer? Let's find some people who are doing it and see what they're up to, and then graft onto that inquiry the voice of the memoirist who is on a quest of her own. What's it about for *me*?

I would also have to find a setting: to find my landscape and a set of characters and put myself in a position where I would get stories. One of the problems with memoir as a form is that it doesn't have a plot, because we don't believe that lives have plots; we believe that lives are open-ended stories. So the memoirist has to create some kind of taut line for the reader to walk along. At that point the memoirist essentially becomes a travel writer. This goes back to a deep internal metaphor, common to every culture: that life is a journey. When the writer embarks on a journey, the reader begins to feel the same literary excitement he feels when he's in the middle of the plot of a novel.

So the narrative framework that I constructed for *Virgin Time*, consisting of three successive pilgrimages—to Assisi, to Lourdes, and to a retreat in California—grew only partly from my interior life. My reasons were also literary: I had to go somewhere and let something happen. My inner self and my manipulating writer's self both needed that journey. The notion of pilgrimage is deeply embedded in almost every religious sect and practice. For some religions it's central, as in the case of the Islamic Haj. In Christendom the pilgrimage was always more important than we—in our modern charter-flight, touristic selves—sometimes know. I could even make an argument that English narrative writing is founded on the concept of the pilgrimage because of *The Canterbury Tales*. It has the pull of the ages.

I went first to Assisi. I had already begun to be invested in Franciscanism. One of the things about the Catholic Church is that you have different flavors to choose from, which are delineated by the different orders. These different styles are called charisms—ways of loving. One story the Franciscans love to tell is that if you go to a Benedictine house they take you right away to the chapel, because they're so proud of their liturgical life. If you go to a Dominican house they take you to the library, because they're so proud of their intellectual life.

But if you go to a Franciscan monastery they take you to the kitchen. Their charism is earthy. This is where we eat and drink and laugh, where we are deeply connected to this troubadour saint. I don't think there's a more appealing saint in the whole canon than Francis; he's everybody's saint—there's a good reason why it's Francis whose statue is in everybody's garden. He's also the saint of the environmental and ecological movement. And he's also a poet, the morning star of the Renaissance. All anthologies of Italian poetry begin with his "Canticle of the Creatures." His inclusiveness appeals to anybody who loves the Dionysian instead of the Appollonian, who still has affection for hippies. I was particularly drawn to the arc of his life—the rebellious youth who is out to make his way and who has a turnaround and becomes the troubadour of the Lord.

There's a tradition all over the world, but particularly in Italy, of monasteries having a wing where visitors can stay. It goes back to the Middle Ages, but it also suits their present need to support themselves with tourist dollars. So I went to Assisi and lived in a Poor Clare monastery; the name comes from Saint Clare of Assisi, who founded the women's order of Franciscan contemplative life. My room wasn't in the wing where the nuns lived, but I ate near them and went to their chapel and walked in their garden. This is what pilgrimage is all about: to visit a place that has been made sacred at some earlier time. I was very aware that I was walking on the ground where Francis and Clare had walked.

I went to Assisi every summer for five or six years and lived in the monastery. Then, for the first section of my book, called "Faith," I collapsed those summers into one narrative, including a walking tour that I made with a group of English agnostics who were hiking through Umbria to Assisi. Of course I left a great deal out. What I realized was that I was in serious danger of writing a whole book about Franciscanism. The journalistic part of me got so interested in this subculture I'd fallen into that I would attend all kinds of Franciscan events. But none of them ended up in the book. The central thread had to be constantly pulled tight.

Part Two of my book is called "Miracles." I thought there was something miraculous, for good or for bad, in the very nature of religion. Miracles exist on the cusp between what we know and what we don't know, between what can be said and what is unsayable. Which is also true of poetry. So, again, I needed to go to a place—a place connected with miracles. That was a harder choice. Saint Francis had been an easy choice; I loved him and he fit into my story in many different ways. But as a late-twentieth-century American I'm turned off by the idea of miracles; my least favorite part of Catholicism is its insistence on the miraculous. (Actually, I have many least favorite parts.) Yet I needed that astringent relationship with the miraculous. I wanted the book to be true to my disbelief as well as to my deep attachment to the pursuit of faith. Many people confuse faith with certainty—which is the last thing I associate it with. Faith has to do with the times we live in. I live when I live, and my world is mostly secular; it's uncertain and agnostic. As a writer I bring all that with me, not as a problem but as part of the whole coloring of who I am. I wanted to tackle the notion of miracles that the modern age finds so repellent.

Where should I go? Well, there are miracles all over the place that are constantly building malls to themselves. The Virgin is appearing on the sides of taco shops all over Latin America. But essentially there's Fatima in Portugal, and there's Metagorgia in Yugoslavia—that's the current favorite—and there's Lourdes. I chose Lourdes, partly because I speak a little French and partly because, if I wasn't willing to go to Yugoslavia and see the latest heated-up shrine, I should go to the most established site. The Virgin is said to have appeared to Bernadette at Lourdes in 1858, so they've had a century and a half to get their tourism down.

At Lourdes I allowed the experience to create the story for me. My own response to being there was the story. That turned out to be the hardest part of the book to live—not the hardest part to write—because of my dislike of what I encountered. But in the end it's one of the most lighthearted sections, because I let myself have fun with it, and in the end I surprised myself by being moved by the faith of other people. I observed two things. First, I observed what was going on around me in that unbelievable carnival of tourism. It was the K-Mart of Catholicism; you could buy candies in the shape of the Virgin— little holy candies—and T-shirts and dozens of other souvenirs. I spent all my time just taking notes. But I was also forced to observe myself in relationship to the carnival. That wasn't a pretty sight. I spent a lot of time curled up in my hotel bed, either reading a book or thinking, "Can I go down to dinner now?"—just trying to stay away from the whole scene, until finally I did go to a number of the processions that are the central events of each day.

Looked at in one way, Lourdes is grotesque. But it's also heartbreaking, because it's a place of healing. The miracles that people are looking for aren't magic acts; they're looking to be cured. So you have more dying and suffering people per square inch in Lourdes than maybe anywhere else in the world. That's the part I had forgotten; why I hadn't thought of it before I don't know. Wherever you go, in the hotel dining room or on the streets, there are people in wheelchairs and on all kinds of trolleys and dollies and other mechanisms. Every age, every debility. Many young men from America dying of AIDS were there. I'm sure I was curled up on my bed partly to avoid all that, not just to avoid the scenes of consumerism, which were comic.

The suffering wasn't comic. So, on my last night, I dragged myself down to the candlelight procession. I was leaning against a tree, watching it, not really taking part in it like everybody else, but saying the rosary and mildly participating, and suddenly I noticed a man doing the same thing. He was a priest, with a Roman collar, and he had the same look on his face that I had in my heart, which was disbelief at the power of something indescribable being released in that open-air mass of people. What we both understood at that moment was that the miracle was that people were allowing themselves to be so open in their need—the need to be healed. There was a willingness to cry out and to say "I want." Against my will, there was something stunningly beautiful about it. So I just stood and looked at it, holding my candle, and I thought, "O.K., I get it, but I don't know if I can express it." At that point my job as a writer was to try to express the almost invisible hinge between cynicism about such things and a recognition that it was something extraordinary. To me it was the ultimate proof of the human instinct to reach out. That's the whole point of contemplative life: the reaching that goes just beyond articulation.

After Lourdes I was aware that all that running around had to end. The drama of a search requires that a moment come when you're not running around anymore. And what do professional contemplatives do? They stay in one place. They spend their time moving around the cycle of prayers and the cycle of meditation. That's what I would also have to do. The final section of my book would be called "Silence."

I take very seriously our habit in America of thinking East to West: when you arrive at the Pacific Rim you've reached the end. So I thought: I want to be at the edge of America at the end of this book, because that will read to Americans as that kind of arrival moment. As it happened, I knew of a women's Cistercian monastery way up on what is called the Lost Coast of northern California. I liked the idea of ending my book in a place named "Lost." They have a program at this monastery whereby you can come and be a visitor and go on retreat: very northern California.

It also happened that Thomas Merton, who became the father of American spiritual autobiography with *The Seven-Storey Mountain*, which is now fifty years old, had stayed there on his final journey. He not only made the trip to California but added that historically significant journey in 1968 to Asia, where he died in a freak accident in Bangkok. That journey was a stunning act, because he took that American sense of the western rim being the destination and pushed it to Asia and met with the Dalai Lama and other Eastern contemplatives. I wanted all of that to flow into my book.

I also wanted my book to end with a *tableau vivant* of someone actually being contemplative instead of running around. And because I am the protagonist, I had to apprentice myself as a contemplative—not as a nun, but as a woman on retreat. Having the book end on the Pacific Coast, overlooking the Pacific Ocean—that was the best poetic image I could find for endlessness and for a merging with the All, which is what contemplative life is about. Most books, even if they are highly narrative, need to resolve themselves, I think, not narratively but lyrically—

they need a poetic image to contain and radiate the themes of the story. I went to that Cistercian monastery twice and lived there for two weeks each time. Mostly I lived my life according to the pattern of the nuns, which was to go to chapel five times a day, chant the Psalms, do the Divine Office (a cycle of readings), and go to Mass. Besides that, I did some reading of my own and some walking.

I also lived in silence. There were certain express moments when you did talk to the other people, but not many. In general I didn't talk to anybody. That was one of the tensions I was particularly eager to get into *Virgin Time*—the tension between expression and silence. Of course that's also the tension that exists in poetry. Poetry isn't arranged in lines to look funny; it's set in lines to make you stop—to make sure you put silence, which has its own reality, between each line. Contemplatives, in that respect, live poetry. I don't mean that in a romantic way; they have literally arranged their life in a pattern that exists between expression and silence. It's the silence that lets the reality come in.

During both of my retreats at the monastery there was something uncanny about sitting with a group of people who are eating and not talking. You become very close to these people without any information passing; I only learned afterward what they did in real life. I found more intimacy in those silent encounters than in the usual way we get to know people, which is by talking and exchanging ideas. We did none of that. The intimacy was based on the fact that we're all human beings, so there's an inevitability to our connection. It doesn't have anything to do with whether we like the same things or agree with each other. It has to do with the fact we're on the planet together. Pure fellow-feeling.

By our presence at the monastery we also acknowledged that we need to cry out. Even when we were crying out in silence, that created a bond. Many people at the retreat were practicing a kind of Catholicism that I find disagreeable—the old-style Catholicism. Some of them weren't Catholics at all, and one man said he was an agnostic who had chosen to come to this environment in order to be silent. The whole experience was like a mirror—stepping through the looking glass. Going on retreat, I realized, is the inverse of going on pilgrimage. To go on pilgrimage means you're out there, you're going forward, you're seeking. To go on retreat means you're backing off and letting something come at you. I wanted both of those elements to be not only in my book but in my life. If you're merely seeking, you can be just as grabby as the next consumer. That's why *The Canterbury Tales* is so funny; what gets exposed is not just people's religious desires but their avidity and their greed—their humanness. But to go on retreat you withdraw from all that.

I now feel that everything eventually returns to silence, including all the jabbering we do about God. We know that God may or may not exist, but that our instinct to cry out does exist—that crying out is about something deeper than simply expressing what we want. Saint Francis speaks to us from that tradition of crying out in silence. That's why he was so dangerous to the church; he was acting against the monastic model because he didn't like all the real estate that the monasteries were piling up. He wanted his brothers and sisters not to be in a monastery, or even to have any shelter. He wanted them to sleep in caves. His idea was to cry out in the wilderness, and the wilderness itself was silence.

One of the interesting things about writing a book that takes you a while is that you change over the period of time you're writing it. The reason you began something turns out to be not the way you end it. A further oddity is that you often write beyond what you've actually experienced. Language can go farther or can have more intuition than you have in your own life. You write something, and five or ten years later you realize, "My God, I'm just beginning to learn how to live that." So nothing felt wrapped up for me by writing *Virgin Time*. A book felt written, and that was a relief, but the questions that were raised by writing it weren't finished. On the contrary, it was only at that point that I really began to live those questions.

I now think more inclusively than I did before. I'm less edgy and more casual about my Catholicism; it's just who I am and what I do. Catholicism has become more of a cultural fact for me, akin to the way many Jewish people feel about their Judaism. This is true for a lot of Catholics today. As the Church in America has lost its immigrant hold, it has streamed into a cultural awareness. You hear people say, "Yes, I was brought up Catholic," or you hear people who would never set foot in a Catholic church but who were brought up Catholic say, "I'm more Catholic than you are." I believe it.

In retrospect I see that I felt compelled to write *Virgin Time*, and yet part of me didn't want to write it. I didn't want to get labeled as a religious writer, or even as a spiritual writer. In this book I would just be writing about one part of life, and later I would write about other parts of life. But at the very least, a new color has been added to my writing. You know how painters put all sorts of colors on the canvas, and you might not notice that there's a little brown here or a little green there because what comes out appears to be lavender? That's how I feel about whatever I might write from now on. I don't expect anyone to call it religious writing or spiritual writing, but I expect that color to be in there somewhere. I have a new area of human experience to go to. That area is faith.

It helps me to remember the greatest, or at least the most enduring, of the spiritual autobiographies, Augustine's *Confessions*. Augustine didn't write the *Confessions* at the time of his conversion, when, presumably, like many converts, he was in love with religion and in love with what had happened to him. That was the moment at which Thomas Merton wrote *The Seven-Storey Mountain*. Later he found the book pietistic and he repudiated parts of it; it was painful to him.

Augustine waited ten years to write his book. By then he had become an archbishop—he was in the religion business big-time. But his book, instead of being the story of a triumphant answering, is more filled with questions than he was at the time of his conversion and his baptism. To me that's the hallmark of an authentic spiritual autobiography. The questions become more intense; there's more invested in them; they count for more, and they need to be answered more fully, not just by some kind of intellectual working-out, but by a life lived. It's that quality of urgency which makes the difference between a spiritual autobiography that's merely an edifying exercise and one that's a work of blood, bone and the imagination. Forget "spirituality"; it's your very existence that's at stake.

HUGH NISSENSON

A Sense of the Holy

The best description I know of how to write well is by T. S. Eliot. In his essay "Hamlet and His Problems," Eliot wrote:

> The only way of expressing emotion in the form of art is by finding an objective correlative; in other words a set of objects, a situation, a chain of events, which shall be the formula of that particular emotion. Such that when the external facts, which must terminate in a sensory experience, are given, the emotion is immediately evoked.

Eliot taught me at an early age to convey my feelings by describing them so that readers will picture them and experience my most intense emotions. These emotions are from my childhood and my adolescence. They are, as

Eliot said, ecstatic or terrible, and my access to them means everything to me.

In that same essay Eliot said, "The ordinary person puts these feelings to sleep, or trims down his feelings to fit the business world. The artist keeps them alive by his ability to intensify the world to his emotions."

Which emotions? I've been scared of death since I was six. My mother's friend Ruth died of breast cancer at the age of thirty-one. Her death awakened in me a longing for immortality. It awakened a love of forms shaped by the mind and not subject to decay.

My fear of death inspires me to create. Tom Keene, the nineteenth-century Ohio narrator in my book *The Tree of Life*, expresses this in a poem:

> *Is Love as strong as Death?*
> *I do not know.*
> *Is Art?*
> *My Art*
> *Will raise the part of me*
> *Writ here*
> *Within some reader,*
> *In the year—*
> *I do not care.*
> *My life to come*
> *Is now;*
> *Within*
> *This tune,*
> *This flow.*

I found out that I was mortal and Jewish at about the same time. I'm like the joke about little Mary Reilly in school who asks Sam Levy, "What are you, Sam?" And Sam says, "What do you mean, 'What am I?' I'm a boy."

Mary says, "I know you're a boy, but what else are you?"

He says, "Well, I live in New York. I'm a New Yorker."

She says, "I know, but what else?"

Sam says, "An American."

She says, "But what else?"

He says, "Well, I'm a Jew."

And she looks at him and says, "Tsk, tsk—so young and already a Jew."

I was born in Brooklyn in 1933 during the depths of the Depression—three months after Hitler came to power. He dogged my childhood. I remember him from photographs and newsreels: the Sam Browne belt, the lock of hair over his forehead, the moustache and the shiny boots. I remember listening to one of his broadcasts with my parents in the late thirties. His shrieks and the howling of the mob were distorted by the shortwave radio, fading out and then getting louder again. I was reminded of a ravenous mouth, which opened and closed, opened and closed.

I vividly remember Jew-hatred spreading here. One day, in 1940, just as my father's business was picking up a little, he came home one night from his office on Seventh Avenue. He was in the dress business. He told me that the elevator man in his building had said to him that afternoon, "Just wait, kike, till Hitler gets here. We'll kill all of you!"

I asked him, "Dad, what did you say to that?" He shook his head.

You must understand that my father was, and still is at eighty-seven, the kind of American patriot who says without any irony, "My country right or wrong." His family had fled here from Poland in 1907. His natural eloquence gave me my love for our American vernacular, which grew, as I got older, into a passion for our nation's literature and history.

Yet as a kid I sensed that my father was terrified that American fascists might really come to power and kill us all. He never doubted during the war that the Germans were massacring Europe's Jews; it came as no surprise to him in 1945 when the death camps were opened. He infected me with his fear that there's also a snake—murderous violence—loose in our American Eden. I tried to capture that feeling from my childhood by mythologizing it in *The Tree of Life*.

My early insecurity about being accepted as an American because I was a Jew made me determined to master my country's literary tradition, to become part of it, to make it mine, and in some way to influence it. All I wanted as a kid was to be a lyric poet. I didn't have the gift. Instead I became a short story writer and then a novelist. I've tried to fuse poetry with prose and painting to create a new form of novel—one that has the impact of a poem.

Some of the "ecstatic or terrible" emotions in my early life were evoked by thinking about God. My father introduced us, and I fell in love. But for years I also quarreled with Him, the God of my fathers, about death. God said, "Do justice," and I believed it. But cancer and Auschwitz made me pray, "Practice what you preach, Oh Lord." My love for Him, which was mixed with fear, became hate. I gave up my faith. I hate the idea that a just and loving God allows cells to metastasize and men to make gas chambers.

What I now realize, of course, is that I make a religion of my atheism. And also of my art. All my work expresses my insatiable adolescent longing to believe in something enduring. Myths, for instance, are a powerful element in my work; many of my stories are inspired by mythology. On my eleventh birthday my mother gave me an illustrated book called *Minute Myths and Legends of the World.* Those pictures and stories changed my life. I still think myths are among the sublime creations of the human mind; they're up there with dreams. In them, as F. Scott Fitzgerald said, "action is character."

As a child I got to know the gods and goddesses and heroes and heroines by what they did. I learned very early that in the Norse pantheon Odin became the All Father by sacrificing himself to himself on the Tree of Life. As a result he became a great seer—a seer with one eye. Wonderful. He plucked out one of his eyes and cast it into the Well of Memory to achieve an inner vision, to remember what must be remembered from the infinite past. He was the first bard who delighted men with his songs. He drank from a horn the mead of poetry, which, I learned, was blood mixed with honey—the best description of inspiration I know.

I discovered from those myths of my childhood that Gilgamesh failed in the great human quest for immortality. When he realized that he must die, "tears ran down the walls of his nose." I learned that Gilgamesh, like Osiris, Orpheus and Tammuz, Kore and Baidur, and all mythic heroes and heroines, journeyed into the underworld—the kingdom of memory and dreams—and that this is what constitutes heroism.

I descended in my imagination to meet Hela, the Norse goddess of the dead. She's an aspect, of course, of the Great Mother, the earliest deity that the human race worshiped. I learned that those anonymous Norse poets pictured this great goddess there in the darkness to be half a rotting corpse and half a beautiful naked woman. It took me years—a lifetime—to understand that Hela, as imagined by those great poets, is life itself. We sense that life and death are indissoluble parts of a whole. We understand, through science, that because of the principle of entropy the universe comes into being by dying.

"Our Mother Is Death"—that's the vision for which I struggled to find an objective correlative in *The Tree of Life*. After writing for a couple of months I found that I—or, rather, my narrator, Tom—would have to paint her to express her. My wife and my editor, Aaron Asher, thought I had gone crazy. But I decided to follow my instinct, and I painted this image that Tom calls "Our Mother" [*holds up painting*]. When I had done that, the rest of the novel clicked into place. As it turned out, it took me seven years to get it right. But as I was painting her I felt in my bones the truth of Donne's words from his "Nocturnal Upon Saint Lucy's Day":

I am re-begot
Of absence, darkness, death:
Things which are not.

All my life I've been aware of a sense of the holy, of the numinous. I now think that this is not from outside, but from within. The human mind has evolved the ability to experience an ecstasy induced by the sacred, by the unified, by beauty. I don't pretend to understand this mystery, but it moves me and fills my life, and it has since I was a child. I think maybe I've always been a pagan mystic, like Plotinus.

Recently I went to a magnificent exhibit at the Museum of Natural History on cave art. There on the wall was the transfer of an extraordinary Ice Age mural. It shows an immense figure with a bird's head that has been killed by a woolly rhinoceros. There hasn't been a woolly rhinoceros on this planet in ten or fifteen thousand years. And I stood there and realized that thirty thousand years ago some human being was depicting a religious tale. It's a myth. The elements of the dying god that have filtered down through our historical tradition are already there in that cave painting.

I love thinking about that. The woolly rhino is gone, but the human mind remains the same. And so does our capacity to make these myths, to seek congruence in the cosmos and to create beauty by expressing these myths in painting. Beauty, to me, is a very high form of worship and adoration. It's a way of keeping the dark at bay.

I've always believed that it wasn't the Greeks who were the greatest artists of the ancient world, but the Jews. Their art, however, wasn't imagistic; they didn't create drawings or paintings or architecture. They wrote. And nobody wrote like they wrote. Their efforts weren't taken as art, as we now take Homer, but as canonical literature—as the word of God. It's interesting that the Jews gave Christianity the idea that the word becomes God: that the word itself is God, that it's inextricably intertwined with the Creator.

But of course the Bible is a great work of art. The people who wrote it poured all of their immense esthetic sensibility into the written word. My introduction to the Bible was profound and significant. I first heard the stories when I was very young, from my father. Then, later, I discovered them in the King James version and fell desperately in love with its language. One of the things that almost every American writer of a certain generation struggles with is the rhythm and poetry of the King James Bible. Once you're hit by it you're stuck with it for the rest of your life. Great American melodies have come out of that struggle; I give you, for example, Herman Melville and Ernest Hemingway.

For me the King James Bible is an extraordinary esthetic document, one that chronicles the history of my people in a collection of poetry, drama and narrative which has influenced the rest of civilization. That document has a powerful effect on my work; in fact, I learned to write in the vernacular to try to free myself from the influence of its melody. I write mostly because I love my language. Years ago Bashevis Singer said to me, "You know, Mr. Nissenson"—it's always very formal—"we're entertainers." I resented that. I wasn't an entertainer; I was a highfalutin' writer.

Well, the older I've gotten, the more I've realized the wisdom of what he was trying to tell me. We *are* entertainers. And there's nothing wrong with that. Life is filled with absence and darkness and death. And if for an hour or two I can give you pleasure with my craft—can give you an experience that you wouldn't have had otherwise—I'm proud of it. I belong to an ancient tribe of entertainers. Around the campfires we entertain. We make up stories to delight ourselves and others.

And yet . . . I hope that on some other level I'm more than just a teller of stories. The religious impulse in me persists. And I celebrate that.

ALLEN GINSBERG

Meditation and Poetics

It's an old tradition in the West among great poets that poetry is rarely thought of as "just poetry." Real poetry practitioners are practitioners of mind awareness, or practitioners of reality, expressing their fascination with a phenomenal universe and trying to penetrate to the heart of it. Poetics isn't mere picturesque dilettantism or egotistical expressionism for craven motives grasping for sensation and flattery. Classical poetry is a "process," or experiment—a probe into the nature of reality and the nature of the mind.

That motif comes to a climax in both subject matter and method in our own century. Recent artifacts in many fields of art are examples of "process," or "work in progress," as with the preliminary title of Joyce's last work, *Finnegans Wake*. Real poetry isn't consciously composed as "poetry," as if one only sat down to compose a poem or a novel for publication. Some people do work that way:

artists whose motivations are less interesting than those of Shakespeare, Dante, Rimbaud, and Gertrude Stein, or of certain surrealist verbal alchemists—Tristan Tzara, Andre Breton, Antonin Artaud—or of the elders Pound and William Carlos Williams, or, specifically in our own time, of William Burroughs and Jack Kerouac. For most of "The Moderns," as with the Imagists of the twenties and thirties in our century, the motive has been purification of mind and speech. Thus we have the great verses of T. S. Elliot:

> *Since our concern was speech, and speech impelled us*
> *To purify the dialect of the tribe*
> *And urge the mind to aftersight and foresight,*
> *Let me disclose the gifts reserved for age*
> *To set a crown upon your lifetime's effort.*
> *First, the cold friction of expiring sense*
> *Without enchantment, offering no promise*
> *But bitter tastelessness of shadow fruit*
> *As body and soul begin to fall asunder.*

There's a common misconception among puritanical meditators and puritanical businessmen, who think they've got "reality" in their hands, that high poetics and art as practiced in the twentieth century are practiced as silly Bohemian indulgence, rather than for the reason that one practices mindfulness in meditation or accuracy in commerce. Western fine art and other meditation practices are brother-and-sister-related activities. (Which is quite different from the notion that East is East and West is West and never the twain shall meet—an idiot slogan denying the fact East and West the brain's the same.) It's an important insight to have, so that as meditation practitioners and businessmen we don't become inhibited in expressing and probing ourselves through various art means that we've inherited—from poetry to music to tea ceremony to archery to horsemanship to cinema to jazz blues to painting, even New Wave electric music.

Major works of twentieth-century art are probes of consciousness—particular experiments with recollection or mindfulness, experiments with language and speech, experiments with forms. Modern art is an attempt to define or recognize or experience perception—pure perception. I'm taking the word "probe" for poetry—poetry as a probe into one subject or another—from the poet Gregory Corso. He speaks of poetry as a probe into Marriage, Hair, Mind, Death, Army, Police, which are the titles of some of his earlier poems. He uses poetry to take an individual word and probe all its possible variants. He'll take a concept like death, for instance, and pour every archetypal thought he's ever thought or could recollect having thought about death and lay them out in poetic form— making a whole mandala of thoughts about it.

Kerouac and I, following Arthur Rimbaud and Baudelaire, our great-grandfathers among hermetic poets and philosophers, were experimenting naïvely with what we thought of as "new reality," or "Supreme Reality." Actually that was a phrase in use in 1945; we were thinking in terms of a new vision or a new consciousness, after the little passage in Rimbaud's *A Season in Hell:* "Noël sur la terre!" "When shall we go beyond the shores and the mountains, to salute the birth of new work, new wisdom, the flight of tyrants and demons, end of superstition, to adore—the first!—Christmas on earth!" In fact, the phrase "new consciousness" circulated among Beat Generation writers as our poetic motif in the early fifties. The specific intention of that decade's poetry was the exploration of consciousness, which is why we were interested in psychedelic or mind-manifesting substances—not necessarily synthetic; they might also be herbs or cacti.

Kerouac's motive for his probe was disillusionment: the heavy experience of the lives, old age, sickness and death of his father and his older brother, whose dying he experienced as he took care of them and watched them in their beds, close to their deaths. As he wrote in *Visions of Cody*, in 1951:

I'm writing this book because we're all going to die—in the loneliness of my life, my father dead, my brother dead, my mother far away, my sister and my wife far away, nothing here but my own tragic hands . . . that are now left to guide and disappear their own way into the common dark of all our death, sleeping in me raw bed, alone and stupid: with just this one pride and consolation: my heart broke in the general despair and opened up inwards to the Lord, I made a supplication in this dream.

As a motive for writing a giant novel, this passage from *Visions of Cody* is a terrific stroke of awareness and *bodhisattva* heart, or outgoingness of heart. So I'm speaking about the ground of poetry and purification of motive. A few Buddhist dharma phrases correlate charmingly with the process of Bohemian art of the twentieth century—notions like "Take a nontotalitarian attitude," "Express yourself courageously," "Be outrageous to yourself," "Don't conform to your idea of what is expected but conform to your present spontaneous mind, your raw awareness." That's how Dharma poets "make it new"—which was Pound's adjuration.

You need a certain deconditioning of attitude—a deconditioning of rigidity and unyieldingness—so that you can get to the heart of your own thought. That's parallel with traditional Buddhist ideas of renunciation—renunciation of hand-me-down conditioned conceptions of mind. It's the meditative practice of "letting go of thoughts"—neither pushing them away nor inviting them in, but, as you sit meditating, watching the procession of thought forms pass by, rising, flowering and dissolving, and disowning them, so to speak: you're not responsible any more than you're responsible for the weather, because you can't tell in advance what you're going to think next. Otherwise you'd be able to predict every thought, and that would be sad for you. There are some people whose thoughts are all predictable.

So it requires cultivation of tolerance towards one's own thoughts and impulses and ideas—the tolerance necessary for the perception of one's own mind, the kindness to the self necessary for acceptance of that process of consciousness and for acceptance of the mind's raw contents, as in Walt Whitman's "Song of Myself," so that you can look from the outside into the skull and see what's there in your head.

The specific parallel to be drawn is to Keats's notion of "negative capability," written out in a letter to his brother. He was considering Shakespeare's character and asking what kind of quality went to form a man of achievement, especially in literature. "Negative capability," he wrote, "is when a man is capable of being in uncertainties, mysteries, doubts, without any irritable reaching out after fact and reason." This means the ability to hold contrary or even polar opposite ideas or conceptions in the mind without freaking out—to experience contradiction or conflict or chaos in the mind without any irritable grasping after facts.

The really interesting word here is "irritable," which

in Buddhism we take to be the aggressive insistence on eliminating one concept as against another, so that you have to take a meat-ax to your opponent or yourself to resolve the contradictions—sexual contradictions or political contradictions—as the Marxists took a meat-ax to their own skulls at one point, and as the neo-conservatives at this point may take a meat-ax to their own inefficient skulls. A current example might be the maniacal insistence that the Sandinistas are the force of evil and that our C.I.A. terrorists are patriots like George Washington. That's a completely polarized notion of the universe—the notion that everything is black and white.

A basic Buddhist idea from 150 A.D. is that "Form is no different from Emptiness, Emptiness no different from Form." That formulation is one that Keats and all subtle poets might appreciate. The American poets Philip Whalen, Gary Snyder, Kerouac and Burroughs in their work do appreciate this "highest perfect wisdom," both in their own intuition and from their study of *Prajnaparamita* texts.

As part of "purification" or "de-conditioning" we have the need for clear seeing or direct perception—perception of a young tree without an intervening veil of preconceived ideas; the surprise glimpse, let us say, or insight, or sudden Gestalt, or I suppose you could say satori, occasionally glimpsed as esthetic experience.

In our century Ezra Pound and William Carlos Williams constantly insist on direct perception of the materials of poetry, of the language itself that you're working with. The slogan here—and henceforth I'll use a series of slogans derived from various poets and yogis—is one out of Pound: "Direct treatment of the thing." How do you interpret that phrase? Don't treat the object indirectly or symbolically, but look directly at it and choose spontaneously that aspect of it which is most immediately striking—the striking flash in consciousness or awareness, the most vivid, what sticks out in your mind—and notate that.

"Direct treatment of the 'thing' whether subjective or objective," is a famous axiom or principle that Pound pronounced around 1912. He derived that American application of twentieth-century insight from his study of Chinese Confucian, Taoist and Japanese Buddhist poetry. There was a Buddhist infusion into Western culture at the end of the nineteenth century, both in painting and in poetry. Pound, as many of you know, put in order the papers of "the late professor Ernest Fenellosa," the celebrated essay on "The Chinese Written Character as a Medium for Poetry." Fenellosa/Pound pointed out that in Chinese you were able to have a "direct treatment" of the object because the object was pictorially there via hieroglyph. Pound recommended the adaptation of the same idea: the Chinese poetic method as a corrective to the conceptual vagueness and sentimental abstraction of Western poetry. In a way he was asking for the intercession of the *bodhisattvas* of Buddhist poetry into Western poetics because he was calling for direct perception, direct contact without intervening conceptualization, a clear seeing attentiveness, which, as you may remember, echoing in your brain, is supposed to be one of the marks of Zen masters, as in their practice of gardening, tea ceremony, flower arranging or archery.

That idea was relatively rare in late-nineteenth-century academic Western poetry, though Pound also drew from advanced Western models—old Dante to the French modernist poets Jules Laforgue, Tristan Corbière and Rimbaud. The tradition was initiated by Baudelaire, who had updated the poetic consciousness of the nineteenth century to include the city, real estate, houses, carriages, traffic, machinery. As Walt Whitman said, Bring the muse into the kitchen. Drag the muse into the kitchen? "She's there, installed amidst the kitchenware."

Another slogan that evolved around the same time as Pound's and with the same motif was William Carlos Williams's famous "No ideas but in things." He repeats it in his epic *Paterson,* a little more clearly for those who haven't understood: "No ideas but in facts." Just the facts, ma'am. Don't give us your editorial; no general ideas. Just "give me a for instance"—correlate the conception with a real process or a particular action or a concrete thing, localized, immediate, palpable, practicable, involving direct sense contact.

In one of the immortal bard's lyrics, divine Shakespeare gives you nothing but things:

When icicles hang by the wall
And Dick the shepherd blows his nail
And Tom bears logs into the hall,
And milk comes frozen home in pail . . .
And Marian's nose looks red and raw. . . .

That was Shakespeare's vivid presentation of unmistakable winter. You don't need to make the generalization if you give the particular instances. A poet is like a Sherlock Holmes, assembling the phalanx of data from which to draw his editorial conclusion. William James's notion was of "the solidity of specificity." Kerouac's phrase for it was, "Details are the life of prose." To have it you've got to have "direct treatment of the thing." And that requires direct perception—mind capable of awareness, uncluttered by abstraction, the veil of conceptions parted to reveal significant details of the world's stage.

William has another way of saying it—homely advice to young poets and American art practitioners: "Write about things that are close to the nose." There's a poem of his, much quoted by Buddhist poets, called "Thursday." Does anybody know that little eight-or-nine-line "Thursday"? It goes like this:

I have had my dream—like others—
and it has come to nothing, so that
I remain now carelessly
with feet planted on the ground
and look up at the sky—
feeling my clothes about me,
the weight of my body in my shoes,
the rim of my hat, air passing in and out
at my nose—and decide to dream no more.

Just try! Actually that one single poem is the intersection between the mind of meditation—the discipline of meditation, letting go of thoughts—and the Yankee practice of poetry after William James, where the poet is standing there, feeling the weight of his body in his shoes, aware of the air passing in and out of his nose. And since the title of this series of talks is "Spiritual Quests" we might make a little footnote here that "spirit" comes from the Latin *spiritus*, which means "breathing," and that the spiritual practices of the East are primarily involved with meditation, and that meditation practices usually begin with trying to increase one's awareness of the space around you, beginning with the fact that you're breathing. So generally you follow your breath, in Zen or in Tibetan style. It's a question of following the breath out from the tip of the nose to the end of the breath and then following it back into the stomach, perhaps, or the lower abdomen. So it's sort of charming that Williams arrived at this concept on his own: "air passing in and out at my nose—and decide to dream no more."

Another Pound phrase that leads the mind toward direct treatment of the thing, or clear seeing, is: "The natural object is always the adequate symbol." You don't have to go chasing after far-fetched symbols because direct perception will propose efficient language to you. And that relates to another very interesting statement, by the Tibetan lama poet Chögyam Trungpa: "Things are symbols of themselves." Pound means that the natural object is identical with what it is you're trying to symbolize in any case. Trungpa is saying that if you directly perceive a thing it's completely there, completely itself, completely revelatory of the eternal universe that it's in, or of your mind as it is.

In Kerouac's set of thirty slogans called "Belief & Technique for Modern Prose" there are a few mind-arrows, or mind-pointers, which are instructions on how to focus in, how to direct your mind to see things, whether it's "an old teacup in memory," or whether you're looking out a window, sketching verbally. Kerouac advised writers: "Don't think of words when you stop but to see picture better." William Blake's similar slogan is: "Labor well the Minute Particulars, attend to the Little-ones." It's very pretty actually; take care of the little baby facts. Blake continues:

He who would do good to another, must do it in Minute Particulars

General good is the plea of the scoundrel hypocrite &
    flatterer:
For Art and Science cannot exist but in minutely organized
    Particulars

A classic example of William Carlos Williams in America seeing minute particulars clearly, precisely, thoroughly, is in the most famous and most obvious of Imagist poems, "The Red Wheelbarrow." Because the thing was seen so completely the poem seems to have penetrated throughout the culture, so that people who are not interested in poetry—high school kids or thick-headed businessmen—know this as the totem modern poem. Is there anybody here who doesn't know "The Red Wheelbarrow"? How many know it? I was just trying to figure out whether I was overstating the case when I said it was penetrating through modern culture. O.K. Apparently, one-third of the room knows it, and after I read it, most will have heard it:

so much depends
upon

a red wheel
barrow

glazed with rain
water

beside the white
chickens.

That's considered the acme Imagist poem of direct perception. I think it was written in the twenties. It's not much, actually. Williams didn't think it was so much; he said, "An inconsequential poem—written in 2 minutes—as was (for instance) The Red Wheelbarrow and most other short poems." But it became a sort of sacred object.

Why did he focus on that one image in his garden? Well, he probably didn't focus on it—it was just there and he saw it. And he remembered it. Vividness is self-selecting. In other words, he didn't prepare to see it, except that he had had a life's preparation in practicing awareness "close to the nose," trying to stay in his body and observe the space around him. That kind of spontaneous awareness has a Buddhist term for it: "the Unborn." For where does a thought come from? You can't trace it back to a womb, a thought is "unborn." Perception is unborn, in the sense that it spontaneously arises. Because even if you tried to trace your perceptions back to the source, you couldn't.

To catch the red wheelbarrow, however, you have to be practiced in poetics as well as practiced in ordinary mind. Flaubert was the prose initiator of that narrowing down of perception and the concretization of it with his phrase "The ordinary is the extraordinary." There's a very interesting formulation of that attitude of mind in writing poetry by the late Charles Olson, in his essay "Projective Verse." This is kind of caviar, but William Carlos Williams reprinted this famous essay for the transmission of his own ideas to another generation. It contains several slogans commonly used by most modern poets that relate to the idea of direct seeing or direct awareness of open mind and open form in poetry. Here's what Olson says:

> This is the problem which any poet who departs from closed form is especially confronted by. And it evolves a whole series of new recognitions. From the

moment he ventures into FIELD COMPOSITION [Olson means the field of the mind] . . . he can go by no track other than the one that the poem under hand declares for itself. Thus he has to behave, and be, instant by instant, aware of some several forces just now beginning to be examined. . . .

The principle, the law which presides conspicuously over such composition and when obeyed is the reason why a projective poem can come into being. It is this: FORM IS NEVER MORE THAN AN EXTENSION OF CONTENT. (Or so it got phrased by one R[obert] Creeley, and it makes absolute sense to me, with this possible corollary, that right form, in any given poem is the only and exclusively possible extension of the content under hand.) There it is, brothers, sitting there for USE.

By "content" I think Olson means the sequence of perceptions. So the form—the form of a poem, the plot of a poem, the argument of a poem, the narrative of a poem—would correspond to the sequence of perceptions. If that seems opaque to you, the next paragraph from Olson's "Projective Verse" essay might explain more. He says this:

Now the *process* of the thing, how the principle can be made so to shape the energies that the form is accomplished. And I think it could be boiled down to one statement (first pounded into my head by Edward Dahlberg): ONE PERCEPTION MUST IMMEDIATELY AND DIRECTLY LEAD TO A FURTHER PERCEPTION. It means exactly what it says, is a matter of, at *all* points . . . get on with it, keep moving, keep in, speed the nerves, their speed,

the perceptions, theirs, the acts, the split-second acts
[the decisions you make while scribbling], the whole
business, keep it moving as fast as you can, citizen.
And if you set up as a poet, USE, USE, USE the
process at all points. In any given poem always, always one perception must, must, must [as with the
mind] MOVE INSTANTER ON ANOTHER! . . .
So there we are, fast there's the dogma. And its excuse, its usableness, in practice. Which gets us . . .
inside the machinery, now, 1950, of how projective
verse is made.

I interpret that set of words—"one perception must
move instanter on another"—as similar to the dharmic
practice of letting go of thoughts and allowing fresh
thoughts to arise and be registered, rather than hanging
onto one exclusive image and forcing Reason to branch
it out and extend it into a hung-up metaphor. That was
the difference between the metaphysically inspired poetry of the thirties to the fifties in America after T. S.
Eliot and the Open Form, practiced simultaneously by
Ezra Pound and William Carlos Williams and later by
Charles Olson and Robert Creeley. They let the mind
loose. Actually, that's a phrase by one of the founders of
our country: "The mind must be loose." That's John Ad-
ams, as reported by Robert Duncan in relation to poetics.
Try that on the religious right. Leave the mind loose.
One perception leads to another. So don't cling to perceptions, or fixate on impressions, or on visions of William
Blake. As the young surrealist poet Philip Lamantia said
when he was asked in 1958 to define "hip" as distin-
guishable from "square": Hip is "Don't get hung up."
So we have, as a ground of purification, letting go—
the confidence to let your mind loose and observe your

own perceptions and their discontinuities. You can't go back and change the sequence of the thoughts you had; you can't revise the process of thinking or deny what was thought, but thought obliterates itself anyway. You don't have to worry about that, you can go on to the next thought.

Robert Duncan once got up and walked across the room and then said, "I can't revise my steps once I've taken them." He was using that as an example to explain why he was interested in Gertrude Stein's writing, which was writing in the present moment, present time, present consciousness: what was going on in the grammar of her head during the time of composition without recourse to past memory or future planning.

Meditators have formulated a slogan that says. "Renunciation is a way to avoid conditioned mind." That means that meditation is practiced by constantly renouncing your mind, or "renouncing" your thoughts, or "letting go" of your thoughts. It doesn't mean letting go of your whole awareness—only that small part of your mind that's dependent on linear, logical thinking. It doesn't mean renouncing intellect, which has its proper place in Buddhism, as it does in Blake. It doesn't mean idiot wildness. It means expanding the area of awareness, so that your awareness surrounds your thoughts, rather than that you enter into thoughts like a dream. Thus the life of meditation and the life of art are both based on a similar conception of spontaneous mind. They both share renunciation as a way of avoiding a conditioned art work, or trite art, or repetition of other people's ideas.

Poets can avoid repetition of their obsessions. What it requires is confidence in the magic of chance. Chögyam Trungpa phrased this notion, "Magic is the total delight

181

in chance." That also brings magic to poetry: chance thought, or the unborn thought, or the spontaneous thought, or the "first thought," or the thought spoken spontaneously with its conception—thought and word identical on the spot. It requires a certain amount of unselfconsciousness, like singing in the bathtub. It means not embarrassed, not jealous, not involved in one-upmanship, not mimicking, not imitating, above all not self-conscious. And that requires a certain amount of jumping out of yourself—courage and humor and openness and perspective and carelessness in the sense of burning your mental bridges behind you, outreaching yourself; purification, so to speak, giving yourself permission to utter what you think, either simultaneously, or immediately thereafter, or ten years later.

That brings a kind of freshness and cleanness to both thought and utterance. William Carlos Williams has an interesting phrase about what's wrong when you don't allow that to happen: "There cannot be any kind of facile deception about it . . . prose with a dirty wash of a stale poem over it." Dirty wash of a stale poem over your own natural thought?

When I met Chögyam Trungpa in San Francisco in 1972 we were comparing our travels and our poetry. He had a heavy schedule and a long itinerary, and I said I was getting fatigued with mine. He said, "That's probably because you don't like your poetry."

So I said, "What do you know about poetry? How do you know I don't like my poetry?"

He said, "Why do you need a piece of paper? Don't you trust your own mind? Why don't you do like the classic poets? Milarepa made up his poems on the spot and other people copied them down."

That's actually the classical Buddhist practice among

Zen masters and Tibetan lamas, like the author of "The
Hundred Thousand Songs of Milarepa." These songs are
the most exquisite and hermetic as well as vulgar and
folk-art-like works in all of Tibetan culture—classic folk
poetry, known by every Tibetan. But Milarepa never
could write. The method, again, was spontaneous mind,
on-the-spot improvisation on the basis of meditative discipline.

What Trungpa said reminded me of a similar exchange
that I had with Kerouac, who also urged me to be more
spontaneous, less worried about my poetic practice. I was
always worried about my poetry. Was it any good? Were
the household dishes right, was the bed made? I remember Kerouac falling down drunk on the kitchen floor of
170 East Second Street in 1960, laughing up at me and
saying, "Ginsberg, you're a hairy loss." That's something
that he made up on the spot, a phrase that just came out
of his mouth, and I was offended. A hairy loss! If you
allow the active phrase to come to your mind, allow that
out, you speak from a ground that can relate your inner
perception to external phenomena, and thus join Heaven
and Earth.

Bibliography

In the process of preparing this book it occurred to us that we would like to know what spiritual quests by other men and women our authors had found helpful or influential in their own life and work. This bibliography is their answer to our request for an informal list of their favorite writings.

MARY GORDON

The most important connections between my religious and literary lives are tonal. What carries over from my earliest childhood to every minute that I sit before a blank page is the sense of an atmosphere of quiet, contemplation, seriousness, purity, harmony, ardor: a cool, dimly lighted place. And so the language of public prayer with its strong stresses and repetitions is my first and most crucial stylistic model. The Psalms, of course, and the litanies, particularly the litany of the Virgin Mary with its cataloguing, escalating images: Tower of Ivory, House of Gold, Ark of the Covenant, Gate of Heaven, Morning Star. My earliest heard poetry. And the words of the Salve Regina with its mix of official and passionate language:

Hail, Holy Queen, Mother of Mercy, our Life,
our Sweetness and our Hope. To thee do we
cry, poor banished children of Eve. To thee
do we send up our sighs, mourning and weeping
in this Valley of Tears. Turn, then, most
gracious Advocate, thine eyes of mercy toward
us. And after this, our exile, show unto us
the fruit of thy womb, Jesus. O clement,
O loving, O sweet Virgin Mary. Pray for us,
O holy Mother of God. That we may be made worthy
of the Promises of Christ.

(How odd, to type those words. Inevitably, for me there is the echo of the Latin: *Salve Regina, Mater Misericordiae*.)

This leads me to poetry learned not in childhood but in college: the poetry of Herbert and Donne. Some lines to indicate what I love. From George Herbert's "Prayer," the conclusion of a catalogue of attributes of Prayer (I love the verbal pileup of "the catalogue"): "The land of spices; something understood." And from Donne's "Hymn to God My God, in My Sickness":

So, in his purple wrapped, receive me, Lord:
*   By these his thorns give me his other crown;*
And, as to others' souls I preached Thy word,
*   Be this my text, my sermon to mine own:*
Therefore that he may raise the Lord throws down.

I love the understatements of these poems' ends: the definite, intellectual closure juxtaposed against the irrational, sensual mode of faith. Auden's poetry has also been a great joy to me for its strong, sinewy contemporary language that maintains the pressure of the formal.

Prose models are more difficult. When I began writing prose, which I did only at twenty-five, after twenty years of thinking of myself as a poet, I found no models except Virginia Woolf. Now Virginia Woolf is not a religious writer. I respond to people confusing the esthetic and the religious with the same distaste I feel when I discover that my garbage disposal has backed up into the shower; I dislike the confusion of realms. "Religious" novelists were no help to me, however, in finding a voice. Graham Greene, Mauriac, much as I liked them, were no good to me. Their language wasn't what I needed. I needed something more female, more lyrical. More like Virginia Woolf.

Yet Virginia Woolf didn't touch on moral concerns that I seemed, almost against my will, pressed to include in fiction. In searching for the embodiment of the moral, particularly the virtuous in fiction (and I consider the confusion of the religious and the moral to be an even more serious heresy than the confusion of the religious and the esthetic; at least the latter doesn't lead to public burnings), I was helped by the novels of Margaret Drabble, particularly *The Needle's Eye*.

But at the deepest level of morality, the morality whose source is charity, I have been deeply drawn to Bernanos's *Diary of a Country Priest*, although I couldn't and wouldn't try to write anything like it. The sense of the unfolding wounded human heart is incomparably expressed in this book.

I seem always to be writing about a sense of failure in

achieving an ideal, a sense whose tone is, once again, distinctly religious. The most perfect embodiment I have found of this is in the work of Simone Weil, *Waiting for God* in particular.

Catholicism is a way of life which encompasses not only the spiritual but the social. And in that this social sense or sensibility is dyed by religiosity—although it is often distinctly irreligious or anti-religious in practice—it has been important in my fiction. And so Joyce's *Dubliners* has been important to me. And also the delicious comedy of J. F. Powers. *Morte d'Urban* and *Prince of Darkness* are his best.

FREDERICK BUECHNER

Graham Greene's *The Power and the Glory*—I don't know that there is any other single novel that has influenced me as much or moved me as often. The whiskey priest, seedy and feckless, is also a kind of saint because—who knows why?—God has chosen to use him that way. Virtually every life he touches is brought to life a little more though he himself is quite unaware of it. That is what saints are: life-givers. I never knew that before.

King Lear is, as far as I am concerned, not only Shakespeare's greatest play but also one of the greatest of all preachments. What it is about, in its depths, is the question of God, and I know of no work that explores it with such anguished honesty and profundity.

Dostoyevsky's *The Brothers Karamazov* is another of my extra-canonical Scriptures. Everything you want to know about anything is in it, including one of the most eloquent affirmations of religious faith I am aware of, and also one of the most devastating attacks on it.

I first read G. K. Chesterton's *The Man Who Was Thursday* when I was about fourteen and have been rereading it ever since. It is a myth both richly comic and nightmarish, and the scene at the end, where you (and Chesterton too) discover at last who Sunday really is, is a theophany second in power only to the last four chapters of the Book of Job.

Which of L. Frank Baum's Oz books will I choose? The *Wizard*, which is about a little man who is both a humbug and the greatest wizard of them all, not to mention also about you and me as we bumble along in search of what comes alive in us through seeking it? *Rinkitink*, which is about a fat king, a truculent goat and three pearls whose magic I suspect we might all be able to work if we only had our heads screwed on right? To my way of thinking, almost any will do. I lived a year in Oz (1932) and have been homesick for it ever since.

In the realm of fairy tales, try also E. Nesbit's masterpiece, *The Enchanted Castle*, and the three greatest of C. S. Lewis's Narnia books: *The Magician's Nephew; The Lion, the Witch, and the Wardrobe*; and *The Last Battle*, read in that order. If you want to understand the secret of the fairy tale as "*evangelium*, giving a fleeting glimpse of Joy, Joy beyond the walls of the world, poignant as grief," read J. R. R. Tolkien's essay "On Fairy-Stories" in his *Tree and Leaf* (in *The Tolkien Reader*, Ballantine Books).

E. M. Forster's *Aspects of the Novel*, particularly the chapter on prophecy, is invaluable for the sense it gives of what religious fiction can be at its best. His paragraphs on the difference, in that genre, between Dostoyevsky and George Eliot teach a lesson that no one who tries a hand at it should ever forget.

There is no poet I return to more often than Gerard Manley Hopkins. No other poet sees so eye-achingly well, the Eliot Porter of the Victorians, or stirs the blood with so haunting and holy a ragtime. The desolations of the sonnets of 1885, the exaltations of "The Windhover," "St. Alphonsus Rodriguez," "The Starlight Night," the wrenched and compacted immensities of "The Wreck of the Deutschland" are surely among the most deep-drawn utterances of Christian experience.

As to Christianity in itself, David Read's short *The Christian Faith* (Scribners) sets it forth, doctrine by doctrine, as succinctly (yet never superficially) as anything comparable I have come on since.

In two collections of Paul Tillich's brief sermons—*The Shaking of the Foundations* and *The New Being*—this giant among twentieth-century theologians takes crucial religious words like "sin" and "salvation" and shows that they are not the threadbare banalities they are often taken for (and presented as), but are instead rich with meaning about the human condition and the experience of the divine.

Andres Nygren in his *Agape and Eros* distinguishes between the downward-reaching gift-love of God and the upward-reaching need-love of man and then traces the course of church history as one or the other of them has predominated down through the centuries.

Lastly, as one who would be a Mahayana Buddhist if he were not a Christian, I recommend Heinrich Zimmer's *Philosophies of India* as a fascinating overview of Indian thinking generally. His chapter on "The Way of the Bodhisattva" is a particularly vivid and eloquent evocation of those great savior figures whose dispassionate love for saints and sinners alike approaches the New Testament concept of *agape*, and whose decision to postpone indefinitely their entrance into the bliss of Nirvana in order to return again and again into a world of suffering until the last one of us has been enlightened, is a fanciful and moving foreshadowing, seismic with laughter, of the incarnation.

HILLEL LEVINE

I recommend the standard literature of wandering and search at the appropriate ages, including *Huckleberry Finn* and *Siddhartha* for introspective young adventurers. My first girlfriend gave me *A Portrait of the Artist as a Young Man*, with inscription. That I was "a young man" was embarrassingly obvious; that there was any art to be expressed in the "smithy of my soul" was an enticing challenge that I hadn't thought about. But then there was the literature of that "other world," which I inhabited with its many voices. My grandfather's early morning recitations of the Psalms introduced me to words that overwhelmed me with their beauty, even when my religious strivings were not precisely "as the hart pants for the water brooks." The defiant and justice-seeking Amos quickly became my favorite prophet, even suggesting a pen name before I made much creative use of that instrument. Amos Peretz I would be for the not-to-be-silenced prophet and for my beloved Psalm-singing grandfather, the best of the traditional Jewish *mensch*. A family connection to Y. L. Peretz, the great turn-of-the-twentieth-century Yiddish and Hebrew writer, added inspiration.

The Bible and centuries of rabbinic commentary and commentary upon the commentary stimulated my mythopoeic imagination. They provided tools for the exegesis of literature and the exegesis of life. Love of one's own people and love of humanity: how to choose? In that rab-

193

binic imagination where particularism and universalism seek moral balance, God rebukes Moses and the children of Israel for rejoicing over their rescue from the Egyptians pursuing them through the Red Sea: "My creatures are drowning in the sea and you recite unto me celebratory song?" To preserve the plausibility of the transcendental, I read lots of Gabriel Garcia Marquez and Jorge Luis Borges. Pär Lagerkvist's beautiful novel about corporeal and godly love, *The Sibyl*, reminded me that I prefer other-worldly musings of the monotheistic sort.

Books lead to teachers. Teachers lead to books. One is never the same. Elie Wiesel's *Night* drew me into the orbit of the victim and victimizer, as his *Town Beyond the Wall* warned this observer that in my choice of activity I inevitably strengthen one or the other. What better inspiration and instruction in melding the intellectual, spiritual, and political worlds could I have had than Abraham Joshua Heschel? When I talked to him on the phone he would always ask "Where are you?" in a voice that continues to resound within me. Was I on my way to repentance or in the second-floor telephone booth? Neither and both were the right answers. His *The Earth Is the Lord's*, *The Sabbath*, and *Who Is Man?*, among all his writings, are treasures.

Jacob Katz's *Tradition and Crisis* and *Exclusiveness and Tolerance* led me in the direction of history and the social sciences, as did Hannah Arendt's *Origins of Totalitarianism*. *Eichmann in Jerusalem*, her notion of "the banality of evil," provoked serious struggle.

My first encounters with Gershom Scholem and his *Major Trends in Jewish Mysticism* left me completely bewildered but with a sense that there was something to pursue. I'm happy that I did.

It was said of Albert Einstein that when he walked

across the Princeton campus, people were not sure whether he described the cosmos or created it. I didn't know him. But I did know another German Jewish refugee, Erik Erikson, whose presence at Harvard and work on identity were equally impressive and influential among a whole generation with a lot of inner chaos and outer turmoil to confront. From the period of ethnic resurgence in the late 1960s, almost to the end of the Cold War and the shocking rise of the new genocide and "ethnic cleansing" that follows, it was rewarding and vexing to argue with him about his negativity towards certain types of identity as expressed in his term "pseudospeciation." The '90s make me think that perhaps Erik was right.

Of the "children of the '60s" who became interested in spirituality, who was not influenced by Mircea Eliade, his classics such as *The Myth of Eternal Return* or *Cosmos and History*? What a painful shock it was when word began to seep out that this great "humanist" had been an active member of the most violently antisemitic, pro-Nazi party in the Rumania of his youth.

Then, perhaps even now, it seemed to me that one could not be an educated person without having read Alexis de Tocqueville's *Democracy in America* and Arthur Lovejoy's *The Great Chain of Being*. But it was Max Weber who helped me pull it together. There was a period when I never left home without his *Sociology of Religion*. It once aroused particular suspicion, and my well-worn copy was confiscated during a visit to the Soviet Union, where I was arrested and accused by the KGB for "acting with Godliness." Would that I were, I kept thinking. Thereafter, travel and quest made Arthur Koestler's *Darkness at Noon* annual reading, along with Dostoyevsky, Kafka and Solzhenitsyn for commentary.

Never was I the same after reading Nietzsche, particularly *Beyond Good and Evil*. William Golding's *Lord of the Flies* and Albert Camus's *The Plague* and *The Stranger* led me to serious readings in Freud, particularly *Group Psychology and the Analysis of the Ego*. How challenged I was to be more conscious of the politics and psychology of indignation without wholly losing myself in the murkiness of moral relativity.

I have personal and intellectual debts, too great to acknowledge, to Peter Berger, master theorist and stylist, and to his *Social Construction of Reality* and *Sacred Canopy*; to Yaron Ezrahi and his *Descent of Icarus*, and to Irving Janis and his *Groupthink*, for their humane and profound insights into the social sciences in the service of public policy. Also, to Robert Jay Lifton and Harvey Cox for their eclectic theorizing and moral passion applied to and tested on "the slaughterbench of history" in their great studies of the survivors of Hiroshima, of Nazi doctors and of the city as the matrix of secular and not-so-secular values and experiences that might foster civic renewal and religious and ethnic cooperation. These friends and teachers and books challenge me to avoid the reductionism, fatalism and cynicism that are professional hazards of the social sciences.

Other beautiful, inspiring, shocking and transformative readings in my life include Alan Wheelis's "Illusionless Man," Lionel Trilling's *Sincerity and Authenticity*, Tova Reich's *Jewish Wars*, Joseph Levenson's *Confucian China and Its Modern Fate*, Clifford Geertz's "Deep Play: Notes on the Balinese Cockfight" and *Islam Observed*, and anything by Mary Douglas. George Steiner's *Language of Silence* adjured us to think about how the "sum and potential of human behavior . . . presses on the brain with a new darkness" after the Holocaust and its influence on the "responsible life of the imagination." I think of this in regard to the social science imagination as well. Now he speaks of the new confoundedness of the post-Cold War era and of our tragically updated insights into the human condition in terms of the "decline of the incredible." These words send a chilling tremor up and down my spine.

The last time I changed domiciles and had to pack books, I thought of the Native American aphorism about limiting one's earthly possessions to what fits into a canoe. I decided to go to the library and stop buying books. But that resolve has been severely strained by the work of a younger generation of writers of literary nonfiction and journalism, including Michael Ignatieff, Ian Buruma, David Rieff, Timothy Garton Ash, Tina Rosenberg, David Remnick and Philip Gourevitch. Their courage to observe and their talent to tell about the new darkness rekindle my search.

DAVID BRADLEY

This is as close as I can come to a bibliography. For better or for worse, I can attest that it's a list of things that have "informed" what I'm going to say in my talk.

The Bible. Not the damned Revised Standard Version, either, but the *real* Bible, the one King James made 'em put the poetry in. I know it's inaccurate and racist, but holy books ought to *sound* holy. Of course it has to be supplemented by "The Apocrypha" from The Jerusalem Bible.

The Koran. The new translation by Ahmed Ali. I know he's a Pakistani, so what does he know, but holy books ought to *sound* holy, and he put the poetry back in, even in English.

Hymnals, in particular *The Methodist Hymnal, The*

197

A. M. E. Zion Hymnal and the *The Cokesbury Hymnal.* Not just the lyrics, but the music, most of which they stole from guys like Bach and Beethoven.

Elmer Gantry. Sinclair Lewis.

The Inward Journey. Howard Thurman.

Letters from the Earth. Mark Twain.

Stranger in a Strange Land. Robert Heinlein.

Voodoo in Haiti. Alfred Metraux.

Go Tell It on the Mountain. James Baldwin.

Paradise Lost. John Milton.

Luther. Richard Marius.

"The Star." Arthur C. Clarke.

The Origin of Consciousness in the Breakdown of the Bicameral Mind. Julian Jaynes.

The Joy of Running. Thaddeus Kostruba.

On Moral Fiction. John Gardner.

Of course you could include every worship service I ever attended, usually under duress.

DIANE ACKERMAN

I have so many favorite books that it's hard to choose even a handful. So, these are my favorites this week:

Life With Swan, fiction, Paul West. A beautiful, romantic, thinly veiled novel written by my partner. It's about our early years together, when I was twenty. It's wonderful and strange for someone else to be the repository of your memories. The book is adorable; it's full of all those kissy games couples play and don't want people to know about.

The Immense Journey, Loren Eiseley. Like many of my generation, I discovered the mysticism and poetry of science by reading this powerful book.

My First Summer in the Sierra, John Muir. Muir was a wandering mystic who had the wisdom and gift to write down his visions in luscious detail. His journals chronicle a fascinating sensibility in an equally fascinating wilderness.

Man Against Himself, Karl Menninger. Although Menninger isn't as fashionable today as some other psychiatric writers, he had remarkable insight into human behavior, especially the self-destructive forces in people and societies.

Collected Poems, Dylan Thomas. I love Thomas's sensuous rigor.

Collected Poems, Wallace Stevens. I love Stevens's voluptuousness of mind.

Collected Poems, e. e. cummings. His love sonnets are full of surprises.

100 Love Sonnets, Pablo Neruda. A perfect book to give a sweetheart . . . or potential sweetheart. A magical collection of romantic poems that I often return to.

The Complete Poems in English, John Donne. All of the universe pours through his poems. How could I resist that?

Earthly Paradise, Colette. What I like about Colette is that she was incapable of traveling light, literally or figuratively. Even a short trip across town meant packing a loaf of bread, cheese, wine, flowers, a book and her cat.

Proust, Samuel Beckett. A brilliant, quirky little essay that's as much about Beckett as Proust.

A Remembrance of Things Past, Marcel Proust. It's endlessly besotted with all the textures of the world and the joys of having a bustling sensibility and a golden memory. One summer I read it all straight through, but now I like to choose a favorite passage and just let it melt in my mind.

The World Within the Word, William Gass. Gass has more interesting ideas per square inch than just about any essayist; and he knows how to romp and get up to serious mental mischief. I like that in a book, or a person.

Speak, Memory, Vladimir Nabokov. I love Nabokov's fiction, too, but this memoir is especially touching and beautifully written. For instance, he writes gloriously here about his passion for butterflies.

JAROSLAV PELIKAN

I have selected Augustine, Boethius and Cardinal Newman as exemplars of "writing as a means of grace" because each of them in his most widely read book made himself the object of his own study, in a literary genre that has been called, perhaps a bit inappropriately, "spiritual autobiography": Augustine in *The Confessions*, Boethius in *The Consolation of Philosophy*, Newman in the *Apologia pro Vita Sua*. Even more than most authors, therefore, these three deserve a chance to speak in their own accents, before other, later accounts of what they "really meant" are given their opportunity. Fortunately, there are adequate and readily available editions and translations of all three books.

Of the three, Newman is by far the most recent: we will be commemorating the centenary of his death two years from now, in 1990. As it happens, his "autobiography" is also the one for which we possess the most useful and complete editions: one by Martin J. Svaglic (Oxford, 1967), more than half of which consists of supplementary material and notes; the other, in the "Norton Critical Editions" series, by David J. DeLaura (New York, 1968), with some of the same additional texts but with an eminently helpful collection of critical essays by literary, historical and theological scholars. Like many of the volumes in that series, DeLaura's edition provides a good introduction for the first-time reader, yet remains an inexhaustible resource even after many readings.

I am preparing a similar volume of Augustine's *Confessions* for the "Norton Critical Editions." (My late father, a parish pastor, used to tell the story of a theologian who, when asked, after a lecture on the virtue of humility, for the title of the most brilliant and learned book on the subject, replied, "I haven't finished writing it yet.") There are, as everybody knows, many English translations of Augustine's work. E. B. Pusey's of 1838, an important monument of the Oxford Movement, manifests a grace of language that often suggests the sort of English that Augustine might have written—if he had gone to Oxford. My own favorite among translations, and the one I plan to include in my Norton volume, is by F. J. Sheed (New York, 1943).

Boethius's *Consolation of Philosophy* can boast the most distinguished succession of translators into English. King Alfred the Great rendered it into Anglo-Saxon in the ninth century; Geoffrey Chaucer produced a prose version, which Caxton published at Westminster a century later, in 1480; and Queen Elizabeth (the First!) is also given credit for an English translation, turned out with amazing speed.

The most readily available English translation is by one "I. T.," published originally in 1609 but—with the observation that "there was, indeed, not much to do" to correct it—incorporated into the "Loeb Classical Library" edition, with the Latin text on the opposite page, by one of the greatest of modern Boethius scholars, Edward Kennard Rand (Cambridge, Mass., 1968). The Penguin edition by V. E. Watts (Harmondsworth, 1969) has achieved wide circulation.

After these texts themselves (or, at any rate, alongside them) a reader may want to consult present-day studies. Of the three writers, Augustine has undoubtedly received the most attention. Some of the most discerning essays on his personality and thought have been collected in *St. Augustine: His Age, Life and Thought* by Martin C. D'Arcy, S. J., and others (New York, 1957) and in *Augustine: A Collection of Critical Essays*, edited by R. A. Markus (New York, 1972).

But the first book I would recommend for any thoughtful consideration of Augustine's "spiritual quest" is the thoroughly delightful *Augustine of Hippo*, by my friend Peter Brown (London, 1967). It must be daunting to second-guess the author of the best-known set of confessions ever written, and to do so more than fifteen centuries after his death. But Peter Brown has carried out the task in a book that is decently respectful yet never stuffy.

The most profound book I know on Augustine, at least in English, is Charles N. C. Cochrane's *Christianity and Classical Culture* (Oxford, 1944). I like to say that I wish I had written it, but that if I had I would have given equal time to the Greeks, both classical and Christian.

Because 1986 was the 1,600th anniversary of Augustine's conversion to Catholic Christianity, there have been several volumes published on him recently, including my own *The Mystery of Continuity: Time and History, Memory and Eternity in the Thought of Saint Augustine* (Charlottesville, Va., 1986).

For all his eminent translators, Boethius receives far less attention than he deserves—maybe because he is too late for the classicists, too early for the medievalists, and too "secular" for the theologians. In addition to his edition for the "Loeb Classical Library" and his erudite philological works proving that the Boethius of *The Consolation* was indeed also the author of the works of orthodox theology attributed to him, E. K. Rand in his *Founders of the Middle Ages* (Cambridge, Mass., 1928) provided the kind of introduction that only a master of the material could take the risk of writing.

Two books on Boethius appeared at Oxford in 1981: M. T. Gibson edited a volume of studies entitled *Boethius: His Life, Thought, and Influence*, which brings together much of the present state of the art; and Henry Chadwick, with his special blend of urbanity and sympathy, produced a lovely little study, *Boethius: The Consolations of Music, Logic, Theology and Philosophy*, which, despite its formidable title, is largely biographical in its approach.

Perhaps because John Henry Newman himself could write so well—as even his gainsayers admitted, though it only made them suspect and resent him the more—writing books about him has become something of a cottage industry, particularly among English-speaking Roman Catholics. Very few scholars in Newman's time or in ours knew the primary source materials as well as the late Charles Stephen Dessain; his *John Henry Newman* (London, 1966) is authoritative but completely accessible. Louis Bouyer's *Newman: His Life and Spirituality* (London, 1958) is not only charming but provocative.

But I suppose that if I had to recommend only one book as a supplement to the *Apologia* it would have to be Newman's own roman à clef, *Loss and Gain*, which Geoffrey Tillotson has incorporated into the Newman volume of "The Reynard Library" published by Harvard University Press (Cambridge, Mass., 1970).

PATRICIA HAMPL

It's hard for me to separate "spiritual" or "religious" writing from works of memoir and autobiography. St. Augustine's *Confessions*, which I love, may be to blame for this confusion. He set the Western soul forever in quest of its life story. Contemporary memoirists are often on explorations very like a spiritual search in our supposedly secular age. Rodger Kamenetz and Fenton Johnson are strong examples. Certainly Alfred Kazin, in all his memoirs (though I love *A Walker in the City* best), attempts to make sense of a religious heritage in a very powerful and very American way. His last beautiful book of essays, *God and the American Writer*, makes even clearer his passion about religion. His writing—his voice—is the benchmark of spiritual autobiography for me.

The autobiographies of the "great" St. Teresa of Avila and of St. Therese of Liseux, "the Little Flower," are fascinating documents, and so, for me, is Edith Stein's *Life in a Jewish Family*. Of all Thomas Merton's books, the one I go back to is *The Asian Journals*.

I read theology and religious history with a fascination that makes me wonder if there is a scholar-self lurking within me who never got out. Caroline Walker Bynum's *Holy Feast and Holy Fast* is a brilliant—and gorgeously written—account of medieval feminine spirituality that has direct bearing on women's lives today. The current work by Christian scholars like Peter Brown, Lee Levine and others working with the earliest sources are not only instructive, but inspiring: they make that lost world of our own heritage emerge from behind history's obscuring veil. I loved *A History of God*, by Karen Armstrong, for this same synthesizing work.

Ron Hansen's novel, *Mariette in Ecstasy*, is the most

successful imaginative exploration of mystical experience I've ever read—or could imagine. And John Updike's *In the Beauty of the Lilies* is a tour de force, in fiction, of American Protestant spirituality. Andre Dubus's memoir/essays on his Catholicism are important to me. So is *My Grandfather's House*, by the novelist Robert Clark; it is a fascinating memoir of a family's spiritual history. Charles Baxter's *Believers* is a stunner, too—a novel that investigates the relation between the radical evil of history and the powerful innocence of a good man.

Poetry matters most to me when it is a spiritual exercise, even—or especially—when that isn't obvious. Gerald Stern is a powerful presence in American poetry who reaffirms the inevitable search for spiritual, even religious, meaning. And he does it within the wreck and ruin and high jinks of a contemporary American life. The poems of Edward Hirsch and Mary Oliver come to mind here, too. Czeslaw Milosz, in his poems and his memoirs, always refreshes the meaning of religious search.

I'm also drawn to Arabic poetry and to the poetry of Islam, including, of course, that great enchanter, Rumi. He's the one who reminds us that the spirit is most itself, after all, when it is passionately in love. He doesn't let the soul become a ghost. He keeps it in the body—and alive.

HUGH NISSENSON

Thirty years ago, on a rainy February night in Tel Aviv, I started reading Martin Buber's *Moses, The Revelation and the Covenant* (Harper Torchbooks). I reached Chapter 5, called "Divine Demonism," which begins:

> While Moses makes his way to Egypt with wife and
> child at the divine behest, something strange, ac-
> cording to the Biblical narrative, happens to him;
> something which apparently runs counter to the mis-
> sion. In the night-lodge YHVH attacks him and
> wishes to slay him.

I had known that night demon since I was six. He was
the Angel of Death. Was he God?

Buber said that God attacked Moses because that's part
of His basic character; God takes complete possession of
the one He has chosen. He took Enoch away with Him.
He demanded Isaac as a sacrifice. He wrestled all night
with Jacob and crippled him before He blessed him.

I read: "If a power attacks a man and threatens him, it
is proper to recognize YHVH in it or behind it, no matter
how nocturnally dread and cruel it might be; and it is
proper to withstand Him, since after all He does not require anything else of me than myself. The words of the
prophet of exile, 'Who makes peace and creates evil, I
YHVH do all this,' have roots that go very deep."

Yes, this was my God! His demonic nature was part of
Him. He was One! Buber's words melded Him for me
into One Being. He was the single source of creation and
destruction, life and death, good and evil. I looked
through the streaked window at the cloudy sky. God
made the universe in his Own Image: a unity! I recited
the Hebrew prayer, which I understood for the first time:
"Hear, O Israel, the Lord our God, the Lord, is One!"

Another book of Buber's, *Tales of the Hasidic Masters*,
introduced me to a Jewish vernacular narrative tradition
that has its roots in popular myth. Buber's Romanticism
appealed to me. I was flattered as a writer by his pre-

sumption that telling stories about man and God has mystical significance.

Gershon Sholem's *Major Trends of Jewish Mysticism* taught me everything I know about the subject. His other masterpiece, *Sabbatai Sevi, the Mystical Messiah,* inspired me to create the character of a heretical Jewish mystic, who appears in several of my short stories and also in my novel *My Own Ground.*

Rudolph Otto's *The Idea of the Holy* got me thinking about the numinous: that quality of religious experience which inspires awe.

E. M. Forster's chapter on the prophetic novelists in his *Aspects of the Novel* is a good analysis of "numinous" literature.

Isaac Bashevis Singer's novel *The Magician of Lublin* made me realize that the numinous and the uncanny in literature are the same thing and are caused, as Freud suggested, by the eruption of subconscious fantasies into waking life.

Mikhail Bulgakov's *The Master and Margarita* is another magnificent, and uniquely funny, "numinous" modern novel. Myths, dreams and fantasies explode into Russian life.

Jan Kott's *The Eating of the Gods: An Interpretation of Greek Tragedy* is a brilliant exploration of the earliest theatrical expression of the numinous.

Joseph Campbell's *Hero with a Thousand Faces* and his three-volume work, *The Masks of God,* is an illuminating attempt to relate subconscious fantasies, mythologies and creativity. Like Buber, he is a religious Romantic, with a fine narrative gift.

Above all, I return for inspiration to the King James translation of the Bible.

ALLEN GINSBERG

Chögyam Trungpa, *Cutting Through Spiritual Materialism; Meditation in Action; First Thought, Best Thought,* introduction by Allen Ginsberg (all Shambhala Press). Outline of non-theistic spiritual ground, path and fruition, relating esthetics to existential prescience.

Jack Kerouac, *Mexico City Blues* (Grove Press). Perfect manifestation of mind; living Americanese poesy; archetypal, subliminal and witty-conscious spontaneous discourse; perfect vernacular ear.

Feodor Dostoyevsky, *The Idiot.* Dostoyevsky's first attempt to outline the most beautiful person he could imagine.

Arthur Rimbaud, *A Season in Hell,* translated by Louise Varese (New Directions). The great poetic seer's heart diary of his fall from Heaven through Hell to Earth. Basic ground of twentieth-century poetic ambition.

William Blake, "Proverbs of Hell" (from *The Marriage of Heaven and Hell*); *Auguries of Innocence; Songs of Innocence and Experience*; all 100 pages of *Jerusalem*, especially Chapter Three, lines 40-65. All of Blake's writings combine accurate human psychology with projection of psychologic archetypes into visionary figures and landscapes. His work can catalyze practical spiritual experience in the consciousness of readers.

William Carlos Williams, *Collected Poems*, Vol. 1, 1909-1939 (New Directions). Exemplary application of attention to minute particular detail in diction, rhythm and visual or mental observation, to composition of poetry which transfers living consciousness of poet to vivid apprehension of reader.

Charles Reznikoff, *Collected Poems*, Vols. 1 and 2 (Black Sparrow Press). Objectivist narrative presentations of many lives condensed into poignant brief vignettes—raindrops and restaurant counters—seen with benevolent attentiveness characteristic of Bodhisattva's compassionate objectivity.

Contributors

DIANE ACKERMAN is a poet, essayist and naturalist. Her dozen works of nonfiction include *The Rarest of the Rare*, *The Moon by Whale Light, and Other Adventures Among Bats, Crocodilians, Penguins and Whales*; *Deep Play; A Slender Thread*; and *A Natural History of the Senses*, which was the basis of a PBS television series. *I Praise My Destroyer* is her most recent collection of poetry. Her nature books for children include *Monk Seal Hideaway* and *Bats: Shadows in the Night*. She has taught at several universities, including Columbia and Cornell.

DAVID BRADLEY is the author of two novels, *South Street* and *The Chaneysville Incident*, which won the PEN/ Faulkner Award for fiction in 1982. He was a professor of English at Temple University for many years and has also been a visiting teacher at a number of colleges, including the Massachusetts Institute of Technology and the City

College of New York. His articles and reviews have appeared in a wide variety of magazines. He is now completing a nonfiction book, *The Bondage Hypothesis: Meditations on Race, History and America.*

FREDERICK BUECHNER is a Presbyterian minister and the author of thirty books of fiction and nonfiction. His novels include *Godric,* which was nominated for the Pulitzer Prize in 1981; *Lion Country,* a National Book Award nominee in 1971; *The Son of Laughter*; *On the Road with the Archangel*; and *The Storm.* He has written three volumes of memoirs, including *The Sacred Journey.* His books of theology include *Telling the Truth: The Gospel as Tragedy, Comedy and Fairy Tale,* originally delivered as the Beecher Lectures at Yale. He and his wife live in Vermont.

ALLEN GINSBERG, who died in 1997, was one of the most influential American poets, starting in the 1950s, when he and other writers of the Beat Generation began to change the direction of modern poetry. His "Howl" and "Kaddish" are two of the most widely read and translated poems of our times. In 1972 he began the study and practice of Buddhist meditation, and two years later he cofounded the writing program at the Naropa Institute of Buddhist studies in Boulder, Colorado. He lived in New York.

MARY GORDON is the author of five highly praised novels: *Final Payments,* which was nominated for the National Book Critics Circle Award; *The Company of Women; Men and Angels; The Other Side*; and *Spending.* Her other books include a memoir, *The Shadow Man*; a book of novellas, *The Rest of Life*; a collection of stories, *Temporary*

Shelter; and a book of essays, *Good Boys and Dead Girls*. She is a professor of English at Barnard College and lives in New York.

PATRICIA HAMPL is the author of a memoir about her family, *A Romantic Education*; a spiritual memoir, *Virgin Time: In Search of the Contemplative Life; Spillville*, a fantasia about Antonin Dvorak's summer in Iowa in 1893, and two collections of poetry. Her most recent book is *I Could Tell You Stories: Sojourns in the Land of Memory*. The anthologies she has edited include *Burning Bright*, a collection of sacred poetry from Judaism, Christianity and Islam. She was a MacArthur Fellow in 1990 and is Regents' Professor of English at the University of Minnesota. She and her husband live in St. Paul.

HILLEL LEVINE, for many years a professor of sociology and religion at Yale and at Boston University, combines writing, teaching, policy analysis and activism. He is the author of the books *In Search of Sugihara, Death of an American Jewish Community*, and *Economic Origins of Antisemitism*. He has also written many articles on human rights and on ethnic conflict and its resolution. He has taught and administered programs in Japan, China, Poland, the Soviet Union, Brazil and Israel. He and his wife and their three children live in Brookline, Massachusetts.

HUGH NISSENSON is the author of four books of Jewish experience, including two collections of short stories, *In the Reign of Peace* and *A Pile of Stones*; an account of life on a border kibbutz in Israel, *Notes From the Frontier*; and a novel, *My Own Ground*, about the spiritual awakening of an immigrant boy. His 1985 novel, *The Tree of Life*, a story of Protestants on the Ohio frontier, was nominated for a

PEN/Faulkner Award. He is now completing and illus-
trating a novel, *The Song of the Earth*. He and his wife live
in New York.

JAROSLAV PELIKAN, Sterling Professor of History
Emeritus at Yale, has been a member of the Yale faculty
since 1962. His special area of scholarship is the intellectual history of the Middle Ages and the Reformation. He
is the author of more than twenty books—notably, *The
Christian Tradition*, a five-volume study of the development of Christian doctrine. From 1994 to 1997 he served
as president of the American Academy of Arts and Sciences. He lives in Hamden, Connecticut.

WILLIAM ZINSSER is the author of *On Writing Well*,
now in its sixth edition, and the editor of *Inventing the
Truth: The Art and Craft of Memoir* and *Worlds of Childhood:
The Art and Craft of Writing for Children*. During the 1970s
he taught writing and was master of Branford College at
Yale. He now teaches at the New School, in New York.
His fourteen other books include *Writing to Learn*, *American Places*, *Spring Training*, and *Willie and Dwike*, a portrait
of the jazz musicians Willie Ruff and Dwike Mitchell. He
and his wife live in New York.